35444001839827
639.2092 PEP
Pepper, Don
Fishing the coast : a
 life on the water

WITHDRAWN

BAR   MAR 2 7 2014

# FISHING

**THE**

# COAST

D0499432

# FISHING
## THE
# COAST

*A Life on the Water*

## DON PEPPER

HARBOUR
PUBLISHING

Thompson-Nicola Regional District
Library System
300 - 465 VICTORIA STREET
KAMLOOPS, B.C.   V2C 2A9

Copyright © 2013 Don Pepper
Photographs copyright the photographers
1 2 3 4 5 — 17 16 15 14 13

All rights reserved. No part of this publication may be reproduced, stored in a retrieval system
or transmitted, in any form or by any means, without prior permission of the publisher or, in
the case of photocopying or other reprographic copying, a licence from Access Copyright,
www.accesscopyright.ca, 1-800-893-5777, info@accesscopyright.ca.

Harbour Publishing Co. Ltd.
P.O. Box 219, Madeira Park, BC, V0N 2H0
www.harbourpublishing.com

Caption for title page photo: The seine fleet at work, fishing for roe herring. The fishery was highly
competitive until vessel quotas were allocated. *Harbour Publishing Archives*

Cover photograph by Brian Gauvin, Gauvin Photography
Title page salmon illustration by Stephen Jackson, *Harbour Publishing Archives*
All other illustrations by Valerie Farlette
Edited by Pam Robertson
Index by Stephen Ullstrom
Cover design by Teresa Karbashewski
Text design by Mary White
Printed on FSC-certified paper with soy based inks
Printed and bound in Canada

 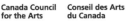 

Harbour Publishing acknowledges financial support from the Government of Canada through
the Canada Book Fund and the Canada Council for the Arts, and from the Province of British
Columbia through the BC Arts Council and the Book Publishing Tax Credit.

**Library and Archives Canada Cataloguing in Publication**

Pepper, Don, 1935-
    Fishing the coast : a life on the water / Don Pepper.

Includes index.
ISBN 978-1-55017-597-4

    1. Pepper, Don, 1935-. 2. Fishers—British Columbia—Pacific Coast—Biography. 3.
Economists—Canada—Biography. 4. Fisheries—British Columbia—Pacific Coast—History.
5. Fishery technology—British Columbia—Pacific Coast—History. 6. Pacific Coast (B.C.)—
Biography. I. Title.

SH20.P47A3 2013         639.2092         C2013-900201-4

3 5444 00183982 7

Dedicated to the memory of
Captain Byron Leigh Wright, Master Fisherman
1943–2007
*Ne Plus Ultra*

Gillnetting before the drum. The lantern, sitting on its float, would be tied to the end of the net so that the net's position could be tracked at night. VANCOUVER PUBLIC LIBRARY 85822

# Contents

# PREFACE

Fishermen leave few memorials. Their working life is mostly unseen and leaves only scattered traces. The ocean was vast before they started and it is vast after they leave. It is as though they were never there. The results of their efforts—the fresh and processed fish we all rely on—provide no clues as to how they have arrived on supermarket shelves. But that unseen world is at once mysterious and, surprisingly, well known. Mysterious to the outsider, as there are few books on the fishing life written by fishermen, that world is well known to the professional fisherman.

What it comes down to is the simple matter of the necessity of making a living. It is not unusual for a First Nations fisherman from BC to fish squid in California, sardines, salmon and herring in BC, and salmon in Alaska. All in the same year. He has seen much and knows much. It is his skill at his trade that gives him his livelihood, and this skill can only come from one source: experience. Until recently, there was nowhere to learn the necessary skills in a formal manner, such as in a classroom. And the few general books about the trade are mostly written by outsiders, and are therefore suspect. There are no books on how to catch fish as a living. None.

I first fished salmon every season from 1953 to 1969, seventeen in all, and saw the technology change from table seiners, which relied on muscle power and powered rollers mounted on the table at the stern, to ones using the Puretic power block, and then to the modern drum seiner. These technological advances brought profound change to the world that I once knew. After a hiatus as a government bureaucrat and teacher I returned to fishing in a sporadic fashion in the 1980s and then more consistently in the 1990s and onward. It has now been five years since I retired, and it is time to capture all of that experience. And in this effort my memory is supplemented by my early, somewhat pitiful logbooks and my more detailed logs of the latter years.

I must mention up front a large presence in the these chapters, Captain Byron Wright, who I fished with on the FV *BC Maid* in 1969, and later fished with on his two aluminum seiners, the old and new FV *Prosperity*. Byron and I were boyhood friends in Alert Bay, fished together as crewmen and were once partners in, of all things, a trucking business. In 1966 we decided to go to university, I to study economics, Byron to become a teacher, and then after a year there we each made a further choice. I decided to quit fishing, continue at university and get a "real" job. Byron made a different choice: to become a professional fisherman. I joined him for several seasons while I was at the University of British Columbia and while I worked as a temporary employee at the BC Institute of Technology after 1969, and had much of the summer off. It was easy to go back out fishing with Byron, first as an unpaid extra passenger ("supercargo") and later as a crewman. To my first seventeen seasons I thus added a further dozen or so. In the end, my fishing life spanned 1953 to 2006, over fifty years, in one way or another.

Due to my later voyages (we called them "trips") with Byron I inherited all of his logbooks upon his death. Through those logs he lives on in these pages, although many of the log entries from the *Prosperity* are in my handwriting, which shows that we shared particular experiences. I was a professional economist and Byron was a professional fisherman, so we both believed in data. The natural place for the data we collected was in the various logs we kept. I say various, as we both had a formal log we kept on the boat but we both also had personal logs and other bits of paper. Byron always had an analytical mind and was hungry for knowledge. As a crewman he drove some of his early skippers crazy, in asking basic questions such as: why are we fishing here? He wanted to know everything and continually pressed me for my early knowledge (such as it was) and the insights I gathered in writing a thesis on fishing (albeit about another coast, the Atlantic). He had a systematic approach to fishing, which I enjoyed participating in. We addressed the fundamental questions: where will the fish be, and when? And more importantly: how many? We did our homework, studied the various runs of fish, made specific plans and wrote it all down. Byron in his logbooks, and I in mine.

As a result, in writing this narrative I have a record of every set of the net we made in those later years. Some of the records are very detailed, others merely a note. Byron's early logs are sometimes sparse in their notes but I have been able to glean much, knowing what he was doing. After all, we were definitely not academics, although our methods fell within that sphere. We wanted to, and had to, make a living. And our planned approach gave us some success.

My objective here is to chronicle my fishing life from 1953 to 2006, and my hope is to show how complex—and wonderful— the world of fishing can be. If my readers are ever called upon to catch Adams River sockeye in the Johnstone Straits (legal), they will have gained some insights here, or if someone wishes to pit-lamp herring (illegal), I will show them how. And by describing specific sets of seines and gillnets in different years along the BC coast I am not only trying to capture a "remembrance of things past," but aiming to show today's aspiring fishermen how it was done. While the effort is somewhat Proustian, I hope it is also practical, and above all historical, and captures what it was like to be a fisherman.

# The Art of Fishing

As it says in Ecclesiastes, "I returned, and saw under the sun, that the race is not to the swift, nor the battle to the strong, neither yet bread to the wise, nor yet riches to men of understanding, nor yet favour to men of skill; but time and chance happeneth to them all." While I don't believe the men of skill referred to were necessarily fishermen, unlike many of the disciples of Christ, the author could be talking about the fisheries of BC, as I knew them. The elements of skill, time and chance were always part of our life, and were all crucial to our success. And success was measured simply, in the amount of fish you caught. Certainly the world of commercial fishing in BC has changed since I first became a fisherman, now so many years ago. But even today, commercial fishing is always about the boats, the fish and men of skill seen against the perennial background of "time and chance." Some things change, some remain the same.

I will chronicle what it was like back then, and in doing so try to supply a clear contrast of the old and the new in fisheries. Perhaps missing from some of the stories about how we caught fish at a particular time and place will be a sense of the pure joy and beauty I found in fishing. Well, there certainly was plenty of both. And you will perhaps find much else in this account of the strange world of fishing on the BC coast. Fishermen may find many errors in my version of events—my memory is certainly fallible. Yet fishermen are generally accorded some leeway in the truth, and I ask for it. What I do hope you will find here is not my story, but the story of fishing our coast: how we did it, where and when. My further hope is that you will discover that fishing can be not only an occupation or a trade, but an art.

For most of my fishing life, I fished salmon; I briefly fished reduction herring the 1960s, and after my return to fishing in the 1980s I fished roe herring and then sardines, or pilchards as some call them. But most of my fishing life was about salmon. I mainly worked as a crewman on purse seiners, except for a disastrous season as the owner of a one-man (me) gillnetter. I didn't experience all areas of commercial fishing, though. I did not work as a troller on the West Coast, I never worked on a ground-fish dragger and I never fished for shrimp or crabs, let alone those weird geoducks. But in the fisheries I worked, I had many jobs. I worked as skiff man, as beach man and as cook and engineer, and along the way I gathered the many diverse skills required in the fishing world. I never planned to start and live my life as a fisherman and I certainly never expected to end my life as one, but then time and chance happen to us all.

Perhaps the best way to start is with an overview of the West Coast fisheries I worked in, beginning with the salmon fishery, which in its early days was the major fishery for BC. Salmon fishing is still a big part of the modern fisheries. As a source of protein it can be smoked, dried, canned and frozen. The big change in the last fifty years has to be the transition from canning salmon to freezing it. Canning had its place in the early days of the fishery, as there was no way to transport fish without ice. But refrigerated fish packers spelled the demise of the coastal canneries, as fresh fish could now be transported. And the frozen fish market in Japan, with its high prices, also influenced the shift from canning to freezing.

Looking at the five species of salmon in BC —sockeye, pinks, coho, chums and springs—we are faced with a dismal picture of stock decline, some the result of man, some the result of Mother Nature's inimitable predilection for change. In varying degrees I have fished them all, and there are aspects of each species that are worth mentioning in any discussion of commercial fishing in BC.

Sockeye salmon (*Oncorhynchus nerka*) are the most important from the point of view of commercial fishermen and processors. Their firm, red flesh, high oil content and exquisite taste mean they receive a high price in the marketplace—and some of that money drifts down to fishermen. Sockeye are in many rivers of BC but the Adams run in the Fraser River is dominant. Every four years, if conditions are right, runs of up to thirty-four million fish return. Sometimes the runs fail, however, for reasons unknown to fishermen and scientists. "Ocean conditions" is usually given as the guilty party. But perhaps our time horizons are too short. Sockeye have been around for about thirty million years!

Let me give an example of predicting runs for that species. In 1989 I was doing my projections for the upcoming season and estimated an average small sockeye run (odd years are usually smaller; the Adams run comes in even years). I was completely wrong—we had good, if not excellent, catches of sockeye fishing in Juan de Fuca Strait (fishing the "Blue Line," as it was called). Later analysis showed the fish were Horsefly-run sockeye. They had been almost wiped out in 1913–14 from the rock dumping and major slides at Hell's Gate in the Fraser Canyon. What happened? Well, seventy-six years later, 1913 to 1989, means it took nineteen cycles of four-year returns for the stock to recover. For a thirty-million-year-old fish species, seventy-six years is a mere blip. I fished ten cycles of the Adam's run and never did really figure it out so that I could make a confident prediction. But then neither could the scientists.

Today the Fraser runs seem stable (if such a thing is possible), but the Rivers and Smith Inlet sockeye, which were once healthy, are not so now. Something happened to them and there has not been a fishery for those sockeye for many years. Other stocks seem to be in trouble, such as the Nass, but it's so hard to predict. Anyone can go through the catalogue of runs and see signs of disaster. Yet sockeye fishermen are perennial optimists— they have to be.

Coho (*O. kisutch*) are also in trouble. These large salmon (northern coho grow up to ten pounds) are favoured by sportsmen for their action on a line. A large troll fishery (hook and line fishermen) has been phased out over the years as the stocks have declined. The major reason for the decrease appears to be the destruction of the small streams favoured by coho. Population pressures, especially in the Gulf of Georgia, meant many streams were cemented over or simply destroyed. Coho are now highly protected and in many fisheries the fishermen have to return them to the sea if they are caught.

Springs (*O. tshawytscha*), also called "kings" or "tyees," face a similar fate. They are the large fish always seen in tourism pictures. While other salmon range from three to ten pounds, springs are the elephants. In my early days we caught many thirty- and forty-pounders. It seems their overall size is decreasing but they are still the biggest salmon. In addition, they do not seem to school up like other species and are few and far between. You might get one or two in a set of the net. They were part of the West Coast offshore troll fishery but now there are severe restrictions on their catches.

Pinks (*O. gorbuscha*), sometimes called "humps" or "humpies" because they develop a hump as they approach their spawning grounds, are a different story. Unlike the sockeye, with its four year cycle, it is a two-year fish. Pinks are also smaller, softer and less red than sockeye (hence the name "pink"). Currently there seems to be a glut of pinks, but their value is low and fishermen are hard pressed to make money fishing them. There are many runs, some small, some big, all over the coast. The 1962 run on the central coast stands out in my memory. Millions of fish came over ten weeks and we fishermen were put on a daily quota. It was heaven: fish Fitz Hugh Sound until noon or so, deliver the fish to the cannery, then go up to the lake in Namu with a pretty waitress from the café. Unfortunately, mosquitoes killed any thoughts of romance.

Currently, pinks are part of a controversy related to fish farms and sea lice. It is contended by some that fish farms harbour sea lice that attack small pinks (smolts going to sea) in the Broughton Archipelago and ultimately harm the runs. The fish farms deny this, noting that run fluctuations are normal. The jury is still out.

Chums (*O. keta*), sometimes called "dog salmon," are fish that arrive late in the season. Johnstone Straits fishermen know that sockeye come the first of August and chums come the first of October. One species you fish in the sunshine, the other in the wind and rain. Chums are large, averaging about ten pounds, and are not very valuable except for one thing: their roe. Chum salmon roe is highly prized in Japan and as a result chums can be an economic species, if you catch a lot.

For fishermen such as me, the seasons had a certain defined rhythm. We would start in July and fish the north coast for pinks, coho and "summer dogs" (chums), as the salmon came in the north first. We would move to the Johnstone Straits by the first of August for sockeye. In the early days (1955–70) we would also fish coho and dogs in the Mainland Inlets behind Alert Bay (also called the Broughton Archipelago) in September. By October we were ready for the chums. Twice in my life, we were able to fish Nimpkish River chums right on my Alert Bay doorstep in November.

In later years when I fished the Blue Line in Juan de Fuca Strait (mostly after 1985), we took whatever we got but it was mainly sockeye and pinks. If we fished in the shallows we got the occasional spring salmon. Our fishing there and elsewhere was governed more and more by strict openings and closures of the fisheries as the number of boats increased and stocks declined. There was no need for a strategy— you went where there was an opening and fished every hour of the day. Little skill was involved, just perseverance.

In addition to knowing the seasons, crucial to fishing success is an understanding of the particular behaviour and cycles of the various runs of fish. Salmon, herring and sardines have been commercially fished in BC for over a hundred years so the stocks have been fairly well studied by scientists. Fishermen have studied them also, of course, with the more specific purpose of making money.

For example, the various salmon species have different characteristics that bear upon how they are fished. The most important species is, as I mentioned, sockeye salmon. They are prized for their red flesh, high oil content and great taste. From the fisherman's point of view sockeye are a mixed blessing. The four-year cycle of the largest run, the Adams River sockeye in the Fraser River, means that the other three years are, to use an agricultural term, fallow. Other sockeye runs in Rivers and Smith Inlets and in the other northern rivers have four-year cycles also. On occasion, for whatever environmental reason, they can even be a five-year fish. I fished beautiful six-pound, five-year sockeye in

1968 in Fitz Hugh Sound on the FV *Izumi II* as they travelled to Rivers Inlet. (Normally they are a little over five pounds.) It was a freak run but welcome.

Sockeye fishing is a challenge in other ways, too. While fishermen receive the highest price for them, they are the hardest to catch. They are a strong-swimming fish and tricky. A fisherman used to fishing slow-moving humpback salmon will be disappointed upon seeing several schools of sockeye enter his seine and expecting a large catch, only to discover they had come in quickly but left just as quickly. He will have towed too long. Wiser heads close the net soon after the fish are seen entering it. Also, large schools are very wild and will dive deeper than normal, going under the net and—curses!—showing themselves by jumping and finning on the other side of the seine. This is only a problem in the Johnstone Straits fishery, however, as the seines are by regulation only "575"—that is, 575 meshes deep. West Coast seines used on the Blue Line are 875 (eight and three-quarters strips, or 875 meshes), deep enough to keep the fish in the net.

Sockeye also like to confuse fishermen. The expectation in the Johnstone Straits is that they are heading to the Fraser River so they should always be travelling south. Not so. They will go south on a flood tide but they will also go back north, on the ebb, unlike humps. Sometimes they will move fast and far, other times they will mill around in an area. This, coupled with their normal trickiness, has left many fishermen frustrated. Here is an entry from our log in 1996: "off Masterman Island—fish acting goofy—set for fish going back." We were off Port Hardy with a

FOLLOWING PAGE: I proposed to my wife aboard the *Izumi II* in 1968 when she came fishing with us for a week in Fitz Hugh Sound. A very important boat indeed. That was the last year I fished with Vern Skogan. UNIVERSITY OF BRITISH COLUMBIA, FISHERMAN PUBLISHING SOCIETY COLLECTION 1532/723/1

large fleet and a monster run of sockeye showing. Most of the sockeye were going back north, not normal, so we made two good sets of the net that way while the main seine fleet fished for them going the other way. Later in the day all the fish decided to go south as expected. Large schools of sockeye were—and are—unpredictable.

Pink salmon, or "humps," were easy to fish. They had a two-year cycle to their runs and as a result were smaller than sockeye, three and a half to four pounds usually; they were also slow moving. Fishing them in sheltered inlets you could tow the seine for almost an hour and they would not back out of the net, unlike sockeye. Fishing humps was usually just a matter continually setting your seine: a high volume was needed because of the low prices we received for them.

There are many different runs of humps, though, so a pattern is hard to determine—a weak run could be strong some years and vice versa. The 1962 run in the Namu–Fitz Hugh Sound area was one of the largest on record. It was so large that the fleet was put on a daily vessel quota. Sometimes others would catch your quota so you could stay tied to the dock and still have fish entered in your fish book, where your tally was kept.

Humps could present a number of surprises, however. The mainland humps (as we called them) in the Broughton Archipelago come and go. Is the fluctuation in runs caused by sea lice from the fish farms? No one can say definitively. Humps can sometimes have a strange behaviour. To us they appeared lost and unable to find their spawning streams. As a result they would lie in small back eddies or coves, or even inside the kelp beds close to shore. They would not move. One spot where they did this was a fishing area we called the "Pig Ranch," outside Growler Cove in the Johnstone Straits. These schools were usually small, less than a thousand fish, but dazed and confused.

Regardless, the overall rule was simple: fishing humps was all about production.

At one time seiners targeted spring salmon. Spring salmon were large—thirty pounds was considered average, though we caught some over fifty pounds. They were mainly caught by troll fishermen with a hook and line off the west coast of Vancouver Island. But we caught them in our seines as an incidental catch. For several seasons I fished them in Parson's Bay. The tide was slow and consistent and the sets were long and boring. In this

I fished with Captain Vern Skogan on the *W R Lord* for seven seasons, including the amazing 1958 sockeye run and the spectacular 1962 pink run in Fitz Hugh Sound. The *W R Lord* remains in operation today as a yacht. UNIVERSITY OF BRITISH COLUMBIA, FISHERMAN PUBLISHING SOCIETY COLLECTION 1532/1242/1 AND 2

particular spot the seine was on the bottom for most of the set and you closed the net slowly to avoid lifting the lead line, as springs travelled deep and could easily go under it. Catches were small—more than ten springs was considered a good set. The strategy was to keep setting the seine as long as there was daylight. I hated it.

One other place we targeted springs was the Pig Ranch. On a strong ebb tide a back eddy would form, and humps and springs would go in there. As in Parson's Bay, the net was on the bottom for much of the set so you could catch springs. In 1959 on the FV *W R Lord* we caught over a hundred springs in one set, for a total of over 2,500 pounds. The Pig Ranch and Parson's Bay were ultimately closed to seines to protect the spring runs. Because they are deep-travelling fish I have only seen a spring salmon leap out of the water on two occasions. You just don't see them jump, unlike other salmon.

But it's not only the various salmon runs that have to be studied by commercial fishermen. It was not usually possible to make a good living fishing just salmon. Also, the salmon season was primarily a summer fishery, so fishermen turned to other species outside of that time. Herring (*Clupea pallasi*) have been fished since BC was settled and have a long history, first as food for the First Nations, then as a commercial fishery. First, they were salted and exported, then a reduction fishery for fishmeal and oil emerged in the 1920s along with the sardine fishery. After almost being wiped out in the 1960s the stocks recovered and a new fishery for herring roe emerged. This fishery has declined in recent years for a variety of reasons, ageing Japanese is one, and the food fishery has taken on a new emphasis. I fished reduction herring in the 1960s and we used the pit-lamping technique that was instrumental in wiping out the herring, and many immature salmon along with them. The fishery was closed for many years until the stocks recovered and the herring roe fishery started. It was, and is, an interesting fishery, for the trick is to catch the herring when their roe is at a maximum size. In later chapters I will talk about how to pit-lamp herring and how to catch them in the Foote Islets in Spiller Channel.

Sardines (*Sardinops sagax*), or "pilchards" as they are sometimes called, were here in the coastal waters of BC during 1924–44 and then disappeared for reasons unknown (it was not from over-fishing). Sardines then reappeared in 1997—60 metric tonnes of them—in fisherman Richard Leo's herring seine in Kyuquot Sound. Since then the fishery has grown, after some birthing pains, to catches of over 25,000 metric tonnes. For us herring fishermen it was a cinch to catch them. We used the same net and techniques. Finding sardines was another matter. But we soon figured them out.

Knowing the seasons, behaviour and cycles of the various runs of fish, knowledge that is most often gained over the course of a career, is what guides commercial fishermen and determines where you set your nets. Over the coming chapters I will describe in detail many seine net sets that I participated in at different times and along various parts of the coast. My purpose is to show the complexity of fishing and not only what we planned, but how we *actually* did it. I can do no better than to repeat what Richard Henry Dana said in the introduction to his novel *Two Years Before the Mast*: "There may in some parts be a good deal that is unintelligible to the general reader, but descriptions of life under new aspects act upon the inexperienced through the imagination." So I beg readers to use their imaginations, as well as my descriptions, to make it all intelligible.

So much is needed for a fisherman to wrest a living from the sea. Nature, fish, boats, fishermen, economics, technology—all must come together in the right circumstances for it to happen. Beyond knowing your fish—and having the right mix of skills and experience to take advantage of their presence—it is vital for commercial fishermen to have the right kind of vessel. I fished on many boats as a crewman. I was mainly in the skiff, the little dory we towed behind us and used for going ashore to tie up the end of the net to hold it in place. The skiff man rowed while the other person was the beach man (sometimes called the "tie-up man," as that is what he did: tied up the end of the net). I have done both. Sometimes I was the engineer and I stayed on deck. I was occasionally the cook. In 1969, on the *BC Maid*, I was alone in the

I fished only one season, 1959, on the *Northisle*. The ship's barometer was donated by Mrs. H.R. MacMillan, at its launch. The *Northisle* was a lovely boat and a pleasure to work on. CITY OF RICHMOND ARCHIVES PHOTOGRAPH #1999 61462

skiff, one man instead of two, and I was also the cook. I put a pot on the stove, launched the skiff, rowed ashore, tied up the end of the net, then went back out to the net and plunged in the water with a piece of pipe on a line to scare the fish into the net. I was, as they say, multi-tasking. Madness, but I was young.

I never quit a vessel or was fired, although there were plenty of reasons for both. The way it worked back then was that you more or less signed on for the season. No contract, no complicated agreement, just a mutual understanding between the skipper and you. But no matter the minor bumps over the years, I believe I was a good crewman. I fished with Captain Vern Skogan for seven seasons on several vessels. Later, on the FV *Prosperity* with Captain Byron Wright, I was part of the crew in various roles for a dozen years.

As a neophyte crewman my first concern was the vessel itself. Was it seaworthy, comfortable, big and "lucky" (very important), and thereby did it have the potential for a good season? My first boat in 1953 was the *Jean W*, a small seiner. As I rose in experience the vessels got larger. The nicest early seiner was the *Northisle* owned by BC Packers, and the best sea boat was the *W R Lord*. The *Barkley Sound* was perhaps the ideal size, a good sea boat, easy to manoeuvre and lucky. Although it was an "inside" seiner, which means it mainly fished in the sheltered inlets rather than offshore, we even fished in Juan de Fuca with a power skiff and a huge west coast seine, deeper and longer than our normal seine. Actually, we were too small to be out there on the high seas but we were desperate for fish. Prudently we never went right

FOLLOWING PAGE: Byron Wright's first aluminum *Prosperity* launched in 1975. I helped load her with pink salmon in Tracey Harbour in the Prince Rupert area in 1987. When she was sold Byron took the name with him as a condition of sale. This boat is still in the industry under the name *Nita Dawn*. DON PEPPER

up to the Blue Line, with its ocean swells, but stayed behind at Sheringham Light (Sheringham Point), where it was calmer but not as productive. Less fish but less danger.

In the period from 1953 to 1969, all the boats I fished on were wooden. Fir planks were placed upon oak ribs, and this was the standard. The boats were well built and lasted a long time. In 1958 the *W R Lord* was fifty years old and showed no signs of age. It had gone through several changes, mainly from a fish packer to a seine boat. The cabin may have changed but the basic hull was sound.

Every one of the boats I was a crewman on was different in design; only a few boats in the fleet were a standard design, such as the "W-numbered" boats in the BC Packers fleet. But they all had the same basic layout: a cabin with a topside "dodger" (a wooden barrier on top of the cabin) for steering and fishing, a

The second aluminum *Prosperity*. DON PEPPER

This is me, 1959, aboard the old BC Packers salmon seiner the *Northisle* with a catch of unusally large dog (chum) salmon. DON PEPPER

captain's stateroom on the main deck and a fo'c'sle, or forecastle, below deck on the bow where the crew slept. The deck layout was also the same: a winch behind the cabin, davits on each side for the purse lines and a table on the stern for the net. All the skiffs were the same in design. They were flat-bottomed but rugged, and were towed behind while we were fishing but placed on deck when we were not fishing. All the rigging was the same. You could go aboard any boat and it would all be familiar.

In the 1970s boats started to be made of steel and aluminum. In addition, the engines became more powerful. In the early days the *Moresby III* had an 88 horsepower Caterpillar, the *Jean W* a 74 hp Gardner and the *W R Lord* a 135 hp Caterpillar. The *Walter M* was unique in that it had an old heavy-duty Atlas Imperial rated at 85 hp, but it soon had a modern high-speed GM ("screaming Jimmy") with 150 hp. The modern boats also had any number of refinements: hydraulic power for the winches, better sounders, more powerful radios, radar and Loran direction finders (soon to be outmoded with the arrival of GPS).

I left Captain Byron Wright's *BC Maid* in 1969 and when I returned to fishing in 1985 on his first *Prosperity* (launched in 1975), fishing had changed and so had the boats. This *Prosperity* was among the first Shore Shipyards boats built of aluminum. Everything was bigger and stronger. Aluminum and steel had come into their own. The second *Prosperity* (launched in 1990) had, from my early experience, everything a crewman could wish for. A bunk for me on the main deck in a separate cabin, a flush toilet, a hot shower and padded seats in the galley. The same high standard of improvements was seen on deck and in the pilot-house. We had two radars (one with a plotter, which plotted the vessel's track and allowed you to see where you had been—it was highly useful in fog), two sounders, two sonars, a GPS and ten, I repeat, ten radios. The engine room was fitted out with a 150 horsepower auxiliary for running the RSW (refrigerated sea water) system and the stern and bow thrusters. The thrusters allowed the boat to turn on a proverbial dime. The main engine had over 600 hp. A small genset (electric generator) supplied 110-volt power for computers and the galley toaster. We had a wealth of power and different systems to make fishing super-efficient. To put it in perspective, our modern power skiff had more horse-power than any of the early boats I fished on.

You may wonder whether the descriptions and information in the coming chapters could be of any use to modern fishermen. Some of it may not, but the thinking behind what we did in catching fish will I hope provide some useful lessons. As I said, there is no book or technical manual that will teach you everything you need to know about commercial fishing. When a skipper takes the wheel of a fish boat he has only his own experience, skill and acquired knowledge to guide him. There is only one school, the age-old one: the school of hard knocks. While fishermen starting out today may find only a little here they recognize and can use, old-time fishermen may have their memory refreshed and an appreciation of how we did it and why. They may also be pleased someone has told it like it was for them. For ordinary readers—meaning any non-fishermen!—I can merely chronicle how it was for me and my skippers and shipmates. I fished for a living and a life, but now I see it was, in its larger sense, an art. The art of fishing is to be found herein. I hope you find it.

Thompson Nicola Regional District Library System

## CHAPTER ONE

# EARLY DAYS

**W**hen the first European settlers came to BC they found a country full of resources. The wealth was unimaginable. Of primary interest were the furs, from beaver on land and fur seals in the ocean. But they could not help but notice the salmon as well and a fishing industry soon emerged, mostly concentrated on the Fraser River. The industry quickly expanded up the coast to include Rivers and Smith Inlets and other northern areas. Close to my island home in Alert Bay, 180 miles (290 kilometres) from Vancouver, a small fishery was established in the Nimpkish River on Vancouver Island in the 1900s. The salmon were caught and then salted across the strait at a small facility on Cormorant Island, soon to be a Native reserve and ultimately the village of Alert Bay. By 1941, the year my family and I came to Alert Bay, BC Packers had a cannery and a herring reduction plant located in the middle of the village. The life of the village was based on fishing.

For workers, the BC Packers cannery had a Chinese work gang with their own cookhouse, women and men from the village, and managers, foremen, accountants, storekeepers, a net loft boss and others to run it all. The cannery was the major employer

The reserve in Alert Bay around 1938. The cedar beams of the longhouse are long since gone, but they were still standing when I arrived in 1941. IMAGE AA-00175 COURTESY OF ROYAL BC MUSEUM, BC ARCHIVES

on the island. The village itself was also the administrative centre for the large surrounding area, mostly logging camps and remote First Nations villages. The island was home to a government Fisheries office with a small vessel, the *Black Raven*, a forestry office with a vessel as well, and a game warden, without one. Alert Bay had a telegraph office, a police station (provincial, not RCMP), several stores, a small Chinese community, two shipyards (one was Japanese-Canadian) and a few machine shops. In addition, the Columbia Coast Mission, from England, ran a small hospital, St George's. All in all, it was a thriving coastal community. The only connection with the outside world was by boat. Union Steamships supplied almost all the freight and passenger service on the coast.

My family arrived in Alert Bay on March 1, 1941, my father to be the engineer at St. Michael's Indian Residential School (as it was then known). The school was located on the far end of the Native reserve. It was operated jointly by the federal Department of Indian Affairs and the Anglican Church. The school had over two hundred students from all over the coast. For the educational plan, as it was called, there were teachers, a farmer, various supervisors and the required religious instruction from the Anglican Church of Canada. My father's job was to operate the steam boilers that supplied heat and hot water to the school, as well as to perform other mechanical duties.

Both my mother and my father worked at St. Michael's Indian Residential School in Alert Bay. Our house was located on the other side of the older building on the right. IMAGE H-04004 COURTESY OF ROYAL BC MUSEUM, BC ARCHIVES

For many years, salmon were cut by hand in the canneries, but high-speed mechanization would eventually take over and make such labour obsolete. VANCOUVER PUBLIC LIBRARY 2065

St. Michael's itself was on a special type of reserve, called an "industrial reserve," at one end of the island. Being specified as industrial meant the reserve was one where Native people from remote communities would settle in order to supply labour to the cannery and other unknown future businesses. The school's big red-brick building dominated the area. St. Michael's also operated a large farm with about twenty cows—and unwittingly introduced milk to the Native people, many of whom were lactose intolerant. The Engineer's House, as it was called, was next to the school and I lived there for three years. In September I went to the "white" school in the village. It was a two-room school with

grades one to six. In January 1942 the village's Japanese shipbuild-
ers and their families were interned and my new friends Muso
and Goro were gone.

Because I lived on the reserve, most of my boyhood friends
were First Nations kids. Like all the other children there, I was
able to come and go freely from house to house. The custom of
knocking on a door before you entered was not yet universal; on
the reserve you just walked in. One house I often went to was
Heber Webber's—he lived close to us. Heber was an eminently

In 1942, many Japanese-Canadian fishermen in BC were interned and
their boats were sold off. Some later returned to the industry, working
mainly as gillnetters. HARBOUR PUBLISHING ARCHIVES

friendly man, with not an enemy in the world, and also very religious. One day in the early summer of 1941, when I was six years old, he asked my mother if I could go with him for a day and catch salmon. She, of course, agreed.

So on a bright June morning I went aboard the small BC Packers table seiner FV *Nishga*. Several events had conspired to have a First Nations captain on a fish boat in the Johnstone Straits. The war had created an unprecedented demand for salmon, principally the UK, and with the internment of Japanese fishermen the need arose for First Nations fishermen. Who better to fish? They knew the fish and the waters, and their extended families supplied suitable manpower. The crew of the *Nishga* were all First Nations, related in one way or another to Heber. So we left the BC Packers dock and headed for the Nimpkish River several miles away and made a set of the net. I don't recall how many fish we caught but I was fascinated with the net, and how it was able to get salmon out of the water. That set was my introduction to salmon seining. It seemed ingenious, and it was.

I knew about the First Nations predilection for jokes and mimicry; they were masters, and I was now to be a victim of it. Heber called me up to the bridge and said, see that boat over there? It is the Fisheries patrol boat the *Black Raven*. Do you have a license to fish? he asked. I sombrely replied no. Well, we will have to hide you, he said. So they put me down in the hold with the fish for about a half-hour and then called me up to say it was all clear. That was close, Heber said without a smile. I wouldn't

FOLLOWING PAGE: The *Nishga* was the first boat I ever fished on, back in 1941. Here, Heber Webber is at the helm and I believe that is Reverend John Nygaard standing on the net table at the stern. UNIVERSITY OF BRITISH COLUMBIA, FISHERMAN PUBLISHING SOCIETY COLLECTION 1532/884/1, 2

want you to go to jail. I thanked my lucky stars. They had a good laugh, I am sure.

When we got back at the dock one of the crew cleaned a fish, showing me how, and I put it in a potato sack and took it home to my mother. My first fish! A beautiful Nimpkish River sockeye, the best on the coast! I still recall it with that special pleasure that comes with catching your own fish. Sadly, Heber is no more, a good man gone for sure, and his boat is now scrapped somewhere. But he and I were part of the larger events in the world, such as the war. I knew or cared little about those seemingly far-off issues. All I knew was that you could catch fish. Heber showed me that. My start in the fishing world was auspicious.

Years later I used to see the *Nishga* on the fishing grounds and the wry comment was that he, Heber, had an unfair advantage over other fishermen. The reason given was that his cook was a Pentecostal minister who led prayer sessions each morning with the crew before they started fishing. Their connection with the Almighty meant it was not a level playing field. One day in the net loft someone pointed out to the minister that we should not believe everything in the New Testament as fishermen mostly wrote it. He joined in the general laughter. I was to hear that comment many times in the future.

Village life, as I knew it, had three elements. My own life was centred on school, and my mother was a schoolteacher; the administrative class of the village administered things; and island's working people fished and sometimes went logging. If you were a fisherman, you did not work much in the winter. You took the risk of fishing: no fish, no pay, and if the season was good you could take the winter off. Otherwise, you went to a logging camp or simply subsisted. No unemployment insurance, no family allowance, no system of welfare. But no one starved. Everyone put

Wadham's Cannery in Rivers Inlet was one of many that dotted the coast during the salmon-fishing boom of the 1940s. IMAGE D-02036 COURTESY OF ROYAL BC MUSEUM, BC ARCHIVES

up fish for the winter. If you also had a few sacks of potatoes and some flour for bread, you could eat every day. That was the way it was and I was happy in it. Everything took place against a background of fishing. You could not help but be conscious of the ocean. As in all fishing villages, every house faced it. The regular twice-a-day tide constantly reminded you that your life was dominated by the sea.

During the war the village prospered and some of that prosperity was due to fishing. A small salmon fleet with seiners, gill-netters and the odd salmon troller was based out of Alert Bay. In addition to their seiners, the fishing companies had a system of renting small gillnetters to Native fishermen and had many Native crews on their seine boats. The several Croatian and Italian seiners who arrived every summer added to this local fleet. All in all about forty small seiners were based in Alert Bay. Only a few fished the Nimpkish sockeye, as the catches were invariably small. For several winters the herring reduction plant operated and the prevailing southeast wind sent the acrid smell into the Native village. No one seemed to mind, it was the "money smell," they said.

The UK was a traditional market for BC salmon and with the war the demand urgently increased, so every effort was being made to catch salmon and can them. The Alert Bay cannery was turning out one-pound "talls," the standard size of can, for that market. The 1941 season was not too productive but the 1942 salmon run was phenomenal. The war expanded the overall world demand for salmon, so coastal canneries expanded up and down the coast. The Rivers and Smith Inlets had many canneries

The Alert Bay Canning Company had its own label for Nimpkish sockeye, which was processed in the BC Packers plant. The cannery closed in 1954. HARBOUR PUBLISHING ARCHIVES

for their salmon runs. Salmon fishing became a big business for BC.

By that time the war had expanded to include Japan and the Americans. The initial impact of the war itself on the village was overall somewhat muted. A few men joined the army, but most stayed. But by 1942 efforts were being made to bring the village into the war effort. A blackout was enforced, which required my father to make blinds for the windows out of black tarpaper and cedar frames. They were put up every night. The purpose was to confuse the pilots of Japanese warplanes, but they never came.

Other measures were taken. The Pacific Coast Militia Rangers were formed, with men in the village volunteering for the Home Guard. They were issued with 30-30 saddle rifles, which were practically useless for anything but being a saddle rifle. A Bren gun, which was a light machine gun used by the Canadian army, was also issued to the Rangers but little ammunition was provided for it. Sometimes the Rangers practised firing it off one of the docks, at a target in the water. But the major event that brought the war to the island's daily life was the issuing of ration books for butter and sugar and, rarely, beer. Later, meat was rationed. Curiously, this was not much of a hardship—fish were plentiful. My mother kept our ration books in her purse at all times. But when we lived at St. Michael's we received all the vegetables we wanted, even in winter, as the vegetable root cellar was fifty yards (forty-five metres) from our house and the farmer and my father were close friends.

The war effort required two things our area could produce: lumber and fish. The logging camps needed men and the fishing industry was geared up. After the gillnet vessels owned by Japanese Canadians were confiscated and then bought by the fishing companies, they were rented to Natives and then even sold to them. Fishermen became relatively prosperous, in that they could buy their own boats. Of course they were financed by the fishing companies and had agreements to sell all their fish to the specific companies. But the presence of a few cash buyers allowed fishermen to get instant cash (and better prices). These buyers were not connected with the large companies and supplied their own small markets, mostly for fresh salmon. The challenge for "company" fishermen was not to sell too much "bootleg," and certainly not to get caught. The Native fishermen soon became expert at seining and several were able to buy their own boats outright. A salmon seiner was ideal for a large family, with the father more or less acting as the skipper and his sons and nephews serving as crew.

The three largest fishing companies competed for fishermen. It was necessary for them to finance the fishermen, and Natives soon established their accounts with these companies. An ordinary fisherman had no chance of getting any money over the winter but might receive a small advance just before the fishing season, and usually the skipper of the boat had to approve the advance. The skipper had a better deal. He could get credit with the companies, either for store purchases or for cash advances against his next season's earnings. It involved the sharing out of profits from each season's catch, and could be somewhat complex. For the crew it was straightforward. But a skipper would have his own personal account with the company and may have no interest in a net or a vessel. And as an owner he would have a net account and a boat account. The catch-sharing scheme was standard and based upon eleven shares. One share each for the crew (six), two for the boat and one and a half each for the net and the skipper. If a vessel was skippered by its owner, he could then receive five of the eleven shares. Of course, he had the boat and net expenses but it was still lucrative. Grub and fuel costs were shared equally. No one knew where the system originated but it was the standard. Gillnetters were operated by one man, and he received all the money from the catch but then had to pay for all of the expenses.

This increase in fishing activity in the village meant more or less full employment. One impact was that boys left school at sixteen years of age. The school curriculum really had nothing to do with their life. They only needed the basics: the ability to read, to write a little and to count and do simple arithmetic. Other than that, everything they needed in skills to make a living was to be found outside of school. Nowhere were they taught the skills to mend nets, operate a boat or work in a logging camp. They

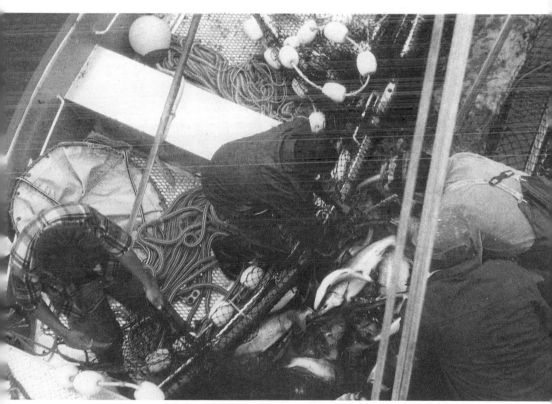

Here the net is being "dried up," or gathered in, to prepare for bringing the fish aboard. The canvas sea anchor, which can be seen on the left, on the floor of the skiff, is used to pull the net off the drum. HARBOUR PUBLISHING ARCHIVES

learned on the job. Everyone had money—not much, but at least they had some. And in fact, their cash needs were minimal.

These boom years continued for some time after the war, and indeed for many years—until the 1970s, in fact, when we started to see overcapacity in the number of vessels. But in the early days fishing and logging powered the small island economy of Alert Bay, and the wireless station, the hospital and various government agencies provided steady sources of income for those who didn't fish or log. And with their increased incomes fishermen bought more powerful engines for their boats. The Easthope engine of a gillnetter would be replaced by a Chrysler Crown or a Gray Marine, a jump in horsepower from fifteen to fifty. People made more trips to Vancouver and entered the larger economy, shopping at Eaton's and Woodward's.

The impact of the war on the island was incremental and subtle, but the net effect was profound. First, the white community was obviously more prosperous, and this prosperity was shared with the Native community. Living so close to each other, though, the various differences in their political rights were apparent every day. On the one hand, the Natives wanted some form of equality or political power and the white community was sympathetic as they were, in a real sense, their neighbours. But on the other hand, the Indian Act separated them. From my perspective, people accepted the status quo but everyone knew it was fundamentally wrong. The increased education and economic prosperity of the Native people and their integration into the economy would ultimately provide the impetus for their demand for political power and equal rights. But that was to come. In the end, the war years were good for everyone in the island community.

Living on the island I could see the pattern of fishing evolve in my daily life. Every year I observed the routine of getting boats and nets ready for the coming season. Daily I walked by the ship-yards, net lofts and docks. So when it came time for me to go fishing I knew what to expect. The salmon fishing season started in late May in the Nimpkish River. The Natives were allowed to take fish from the river with a drag seine. These fish were for personal consumption and not to be sold to the fish companies or anyone else. Several different crews fished Nimpkish sockeye salmon with the drag seine. They brought the fish to Alert Bay and it was distributed to everyone who wanted some. This catch was supposed to be for Natives only but somehow we always got a share of the fish. Some of it was eaten right away but much of it was canned. On the beach in front of our house on the reserve several groups of women would set up their canning machine—a hand-cranked article—and then build a big fire and boil the cans to cook the fish. It was standard food for the winter. Before the canning of sockeye became common, dog salmon were the tradi-tional winter food. But sockeye salmon were preferred because of their higher fat content and richer taste compared to other species.

Later in the year when the dog salmon were running they would be smoked. This was done in small cedar-shake smoke-houses that looked like elongated outdoor toilets. The dog salm-on were filleted and hung on a rack, and a small fire would be started. The fire had to be very smoky and kept at a low heat. The technique was to start the fire with cedar and then add wet alder sawdust or that of other hardwood. Sometimes it was nec-essary to wet the sawdust again to produce the required amount of smoke. It had to be monitored a bit.

The way the Native women prepared smoked sockeye salm-on was a skill that always fascinated me. They used a special knife called an "ulu" made from an old handsaw. It had a peculiar shape. The ulu was about six inches (fifteen centimetres) long and

Drying fish, here probably chum salmon, were a common sight on the beach of the reseve in Alert Bay. For many years salmon were also canned and cooked in big pots at this location. IMAGE E-04661 COURTESY OF ROYAL BC MUSEUM, BC ARCHIVES

perhaps four inches (ten centimetres) deep, with a wooden grip attached to the top of the blade. It looked like no other knife I had ever seen but it was used by many cultures, including the Inuit. It was very effective for cutting up salmon to get it ready for the special smoking they did around an open fire. The procedure was to take the whole salmon and start cutting on both sides from the backbone down to the belly, with the end result a butterfly-like piece of fish. Cedar sticks were inserted along the edges of the fillet and tied in with a piece of wire. The spread-out fillet was then mounted onto a long split cedar stake (called a "gloobuck" stick), which was placed upright against the fire. The result was a cooked fish that was flavoured by smoke from both the sizzling fat falling on the fire from the fish and the alder or fir wood. It was delicious and could simply be eaten by hand.

After the drag seining in the river it was time to get ready for the commercial fishing season. By late June the gillnetters had gone to Rivers and Smith Inlets to fish the sockeye runs there. Only gillnets were allowed in those two inlets. The seiners from Alert Bay had by then finished with the small run of Nimpkish sockeye and had moved to the Johnstone Straits, about ten miles (sixteen kilometres) down the coast. With thirty or forty seine boats moving about, leaving Alert Bay Sunday night and returning Friday night, I was always aware of what was going on in fishing. And soon an opportunity came my way to do it.

One day, when I was fourteen, a friend of mine, Henry "Hank" Myers, much older at sixteen, said, "Donny, come with me and the *Hawk* and let's go fishing." The *Hawk* was a very small and old double-ended gillnetter in poor condition, and somehow he owned it. The boat was powered by the traditional Easthope engine, which was said to have been "designed by a genius for use by idiots"—it was simplicity itself to operate. You opened a little petcock, poured in some gasoline, opened a lever to lower the compression in the cylinder,

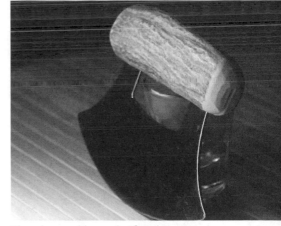

The ulu was like no knife I'd ever seen, and was very effective for cutting up salmon. In Alert Bay, First Nations people made them out of old saw blades—better than stainless steel, as they could be sharpened. KYLE NISHIOKA

then turned the large flywheel by hand. If you did it right, the engine fired. A small magneto supplied the electrical spark to the one spark plug. Once it was running, you pushed the compression lever back to full and the engine would be going at full power. It supplied about five to seven horsepower, which was enough to push the little boat up to about seven knots. Hank showed me how to do it and without much ado we were off. We were bound for the Johnstone Straits and Hank's favourite fishing spot.

Hank was the son of a Norwegian immigrant and a Native woman. Under the rules of the day this meant he was considered "white," although he was certainly dark like a Native person. In this respect he was not unusual. To me he was just someone I liked due to his pleasant manner. We got along. It took us about two hours to get to the Straits to get ready for the night's fishing. Gillnetters only worked at night in the Straits, as the salmon wouldn't gill in the nets during the day. We made some tea—we were not yet coffee drinkers—and soup on Hank's little gas-fired Coleman stove and picked our spot to set the net. The plan was to set it off Izumi Rock and let the ebb tide carry the net and us back up the Straits to Blinkhorn Light, about ten miles (sixteen kilometres). The net was the standard two hundred fathoms and sixty meshes deep. The meshes were five and one-eighth inches (thirteen centimetres) in size, the usual for fishing sockeye. Larger nets were used for dog salmon and much smaller ones for pinks, although few gillnetters fished pinks.

Gillnetting for salmon was relatively simple but fraught with danger as it was done at night. The procedure was to light a small oil-fired lantern, put it on a float and tie it to the end of your net. This was to let you know where the end of your net was at night, and perhaps more importantly to let other boats know where your net was. If you had many gillnetters working in a small area it could be a nightmare getting around the nets. With two lights on each end of the net and many nets it was difficult to figure out whose was whose, and caution was required when moving about. Getting a net in your wheel was to be avoided at all costs, and each boat had a small set of iron net guards attached to the hull to keep the net out of the wheel. The guards slowed the speed of the boat a little but were essential and standard practice. After you set your net out in a straight line, more or less, you stayed tied to it and drifted along with it in the tide.

Soon it was dark and we could see the lanterns at the end of the nets of the other gillnetters around us. Every once in a while Hank would shout to no one and everyone in particular: "Get away from my net, you bastards!" We laughed at this, our defiant attitude to the world and our free use coarse language. This is what real men did. We were fishermen. Several times during the night we untied the net from the boat and cruised along it to see how many fish we had so far. There were not many. At the first light, false dawn, we picked up the net. The little drum at the stern was not very powerful, as it was powered by a system of belts and shafts off the Easthope engine, but it was good enough for us and we had our fish aboard.

What we were doing was what Alert Bay gillnet fishermen had been doing for many years. The gillnet technique had been pioneered in the Fraser River almost a hundred years before. The technique migrated north to Alert Bay and was easily adopted by the Natives. The financial investment required of a fisherman was small: the boat could be rented from a fish company, the net was purchased from them and credit was advanced in the form of gas and food coupons. You were tied to the fish company but equally you were master of your own operation. In the 1940s and 1950s not too many gillnet fishermen fished the Johnstone Straits as it was too dangerous. The normal gillnetting pattern was to go to Rivers and Smith Inlets, protected inside waters, and then at the end of July run the 250 miles (400 kilometres) to fish the Fraser River. I think Hank's father would not let him do that, but at least allowed him to fish close to home in the Straits.

The pleasure of moving from boyhood into the world of men was, for me, captured in that idyllic little adventure. It was one of colour: we left Alert Bay and went into the bright blue sea of the Straits. We watched the brilliant red sunset to the west as we ate our simple supper and then the black of darkness set in around us as we lay on the end of our net. Against the black of the night was the white of the stars and white of the light on the other end of our net, the object of our intense gaze in the night's dark. The only noise was from the creaking of the boat and small waves against the hull as we floated on the ocean. When we started the engine to check on our net we would have the familiar putt-putt of the small Easthope engine. It was reassuring, as it was our lifeline to home and safety. There was no such thing as safety equipment, such as flares or life jackets. We were alone and our fate was in our hands. The mixture of fear and excitement almost made me giddy.

Hank was an independent fisherman, but he was considered too young to have advances of cash or credit from the fishing companies; he sold his fish to a cash buyer. The buyer had a small wharf in nearby Mitchell Bay and we got there about noon. The fish were weighed and counted and a fish slip was given to Hank along with his cash. He got about a dollar a fish so he had thirty dollars for the night's work; he then gave me two dollars. Because we had been up all night we decided to sleep for a while. I slept out on the deck and Hank was below in the front of the boat.

After several hours we woke up and made some tea, and a pretty girl of about eleven or twelve came onto the dock. Hank asked her if she could sing. She said yes. So they sang a song together. I cannot recall the song but it remains a strong part of my memory of that day. Fishing with Hank was my special introduction into the fishing world. I could now boast that we had caught fish on the Izumi Rock drift with no problems. I had a fishing story to tell. That I could not actually start the engine by myself or run the little *Hawk* made no matter. I was a fisherman and had the money to show for it.

My introduction to fishing was like that of many from Alert Bay. Small boys, never girls, went out on their fathers' seiners and learned the skills to be fishermen. There was a convention to follow, as well. You could not get a fisherman's license until you were sixteen, so until then you usually received nothing for your work, family or not. At sixteen, if you were small, you might be paid something called a "half-share" regardless of the amount, but at sixteen you should expect to be paid a full share of the catch. Fishermen all received the same share, regardless of experience. But the work was divided so that two strong young boys (or men) were the beach man and skiff man and did the dangerous and difficult work. They operated the little dory or skiff and tied the seine to the beach. The other two crewmen stayed on deck when the net was being set. One was the cook, usually an older experienced fisherman, and the other was the engineer, who was sometimes called the "deck boss." This division of labour was ideal for a family operation, especially, and was seen on many boats.

Looking back, the fishing world I grew up in in the 1940s was a simple one, but it was pleasurable and had an even pace to it. You could take your time, find your own fishing spots and work as hard and as long as you wanted from the Sunday six p.m. opening to the Friday six p.m. closing. But equally, it was a hard life. No Workers' Compensation, no pension, no unemployment insurance … indeed no guarantees at all. All the risk was yours so you took the rewards as a just due. Life in Alert Bay in the 1940s was all about fishing. And soon I was to fully enter that world, and it was to be the first step towards my long life as a fisherman.

## CHAPTER TWO

# WE BUILD A SALMON SEINE

One bright and sunny day in early May of 1953 we went on a boat to Bones Bay to make a net. We were six: the owner of the boat, his son-in-law the skipper, an old First Nations skipper, myself and the owner's two sons. We were going to make a seine net for the little Alert Bay seiner the FV *Jean W*. Bones Bay is about thirty miles (fifty kilometres) from Alert Bay, located in what is called the Broughton Archipelago. It was once home to a thriving cannery run by the Canadian Fishing Company. Now it had been turned into a large net loft and company offices that serviced about fifteen seiners based in the Alert Bay area.

We arrived in late afternoon and once we were safely tied up at the dock I threw over a small crab pot. Bones Bay was reputed to be a hot spot for crabs, their previous feed being the offal from the cannery. And in that act I saw myself as a commercial fisherman, ready at all times to exploit the sea. Well, I was seventeen years old.

We then proceeded into the net loft. The large barn-like building was used for the storing and making of seines and gillnets. It had very high ceilings and the various strips of seine web were hung up like fire hoses to dry and to prevent rot. Each captain had a locker, where all their fishing gear was stored. We went to the *Jean W* locker, and in it were strips of cotton web, Spanish corks, leads, poles, fish peoghs (single-tine pitchforks) and many sorts of lines. Our job was to take all the pieces and make a seine. Each year nets were stripped down and then they were remade the next year, as they were fragile and stretched and became damaged over the fishing season.

The materials had to be prepared in advance and some important economic decisions had to be made. First, as seine web wore out over time, how much new web should be purchased from the company? The rule of thumb was that it had a life of about five years, so the practice was to add some new web each year in the top strip of the seine. How much depended upon the condition of the existing web and the captain's pocketbook. The same applied to the various lines: the cork line, the lead line and the purse lines. Not to forget my eventual area of expertise, the beach lines.

A seine net is made of many parts. The web itself came in hundred-mesh strips, which were laced together to the desired length and depth. The web was then hung on the cork line, which held up the net, and onto the lead line, which held it down. Attached to the lead line by small straps called beckets were the purse rings. Each end of the net had a gable end between the cork line and lead line that could be drawn up, ensuring a complete closure. The purse line ran through the purse rings to close the net. The beach line was used to tie the end of the net to the beach. This basic design has been modified over time for different techniques, but I am describing here a basic seine net as it existed before the advent of synthetics. Back then we lived in an organic world of cotton, manila and sisal.

First, we had to get everything ready. This involved several tasks: cutting off the old hangings on the cork and lead lines left

This is how the Bones Bay Cannery looked to us when we went there to make our seine in 1953. When it was later demolished, the supplies and equipment were moved to the ABC net loft in Alert Bay, in the old cannery building. Today that net loft is owned by the Namgis First Nation. IMAGE NA-11419 COURTESY OF ROYAL BC MUSEUM, BC ARCHIVES

on after the previous crew had stripped off the web, pulling the leads off the lead line, if possible, and hacksawing off those that wouldn't come, and finally getting skeins of lacing and hanging twine made into balls. That was my job. The needles were of several sizes for the different-sized twines. Hanging twine needles were large, lacing needles were medium-sized and mending twine needles were small. Then the web had to be brought down from where it was hanging and piled at one end of the net loft. All of these were straightforward tasks but I did not know how it all came together as a finished net. That would happen over the next few days.

We started work very early the next morning, getting to the net loft before eight a.m. The owner worked as the cook and was the proverbial cranky Irishman and abrupt with us young boys. No please or thank you, only direct orders; get up, put your plate in the sink and get to work were typical commands in his repertoire. After all, he was dealing with his sons and me, greenhorns in the world of men. Somehow, his manner never bothered me as I was doing a man's work, even though I was not being paid— it was a tradition that you helped make the net as part of your future job. In later years boys did get paid, but not in the early 1950s. We had the occasional break and can of pop (I had not yet learned to drink coffee) and then lunch was served on the boat: canned soup and fish sandwiches and, a surprise to me, corned beef sandwiches. The cook was somehow taken with corned beef, which came in a can from Argentina, and we were to eat it frequently for two salmon fishing seasons.

We worked until suppertime and after supper we took it easy. I inspected my crab trap and had caught several, but I was too afraid to ask the cook permission to boil them up, so I released them. The skipper liked to play cribbage so we played four-handed crib. Cribbage was the game of choice for fishermen. But we were so tired we went to bed as soon as it was dark, around ten p.m. We had to be up again at seven.

By late in the second day we were ready to start lacing the strips of web together to make the body of the net. Each strip of web was a hundred meshes deep, with selvedge ("self-edge") on the edges. The selvedge was made of two lengths of the twine pulled between the meshes on both the top and bottom of the strip. It created space and strength for the hanging twine. Now

Following page: In the Namgis net loft in Alert Bay, fishermen hang a herring seine. Herring seines are small-meshed, which means hard, slow work and sore fingers. DON PEPPER

the lacing could proceed. But first, a technical problem had to be solved. The old cotton web had stretched from being towed, so the ten-fathom mark, which was a piece of white twine still on the web, could now measure up to twelve or more fathoms of web when laid out and measured on the marks on the net loft floor. The problem was what to do: use the actual twelve fathoms of web or treat the twelve fathoms as ten and hang it in? The conventional wisdom was to treat it as ten and so we did. That is, we hung the twelve fathoms of stretched web onto ten fathoms of new unstretched web.

The procedure was to lace each strip to another. The net loft and its floor were set up to make this easy. On the floor were marks at ten fathoms ("a stretch") and additional one-, two- and two-and-a-half-fathom marks beyond that. These extra marks were for the "hanging-in percentage." Two fathoms meant a 20 percent hanging ratio, the standard. The web was not directly hung to the cork line and lead line on a one-to-one ratio but was "hung in." That is, extra web was put there to give the net "body." So on the cork line you had ten fathoms of line with twelve fathoms of web hung onto it.

The lead line presented a more complex challenge. It was shorter than the cork line, usually by about two feet on each end of the ten-fathom stretch. That meant fifty-six feet (ten fathoms minus four feet) of lead line for every sixty feet of cork line, with perhaps seventy-two feet (twelve fathoms) of web hung into that length. The effect was to have more web at the bottom of the net, making a sort of bag.

A simple system had been developed to make this task easy for fishermen. The marks were put on the floor, and then hooks were suspended from the ceiling to about three feet off the floor. The hooks held up the web off the floor to make lacing easy. This set-up also allowed consistent lacing over each stretch. Hanging in the twelve fathoms of stretched web to ten fathoms of new web meant you measured out equal portions of each to each hook. Because cotton shrinks the lacing was not tight—a little slack was added in the lacing to allow for shrinkage and later towing strains. Otherwise the lacing would break and holes emerge between the two strips. Not good.

The two or more strips to be laced together were measured on the floor with the marks added after each "stretch." Usually an identifying piece of white twine was tied into the selvedge (the web was tarred and therefore black) at the "percentage" fathom mark. The web was then picked up and hung on the first and last hooks. Then the centre of the web was hung on the middle hook, and the rest was quartered and hung on those hooks. Doing so provided a visual clue to the men lacing, as to how to lace the two edges together, because it showed how much to pick up between the hooks if there were any differences between the two strips being laced. Lacing could now begin.

I watched it all with fascination and even wrote down the information on an old cigarette package. One of my jobs was to keep a count of the stretches as lacing began. As noted, my other job was to keep the lacing needles filled. I took the skeins, banged them on a piece of iron to loosen the tar, pulled the lacing twine into big balls and then filled the needles. I couldn't fall behind, as the lacers would stop work. Two men laced while us boys filled needles, trimmed the cork and lead lines of old hangings, and punched "tight" leads. These leads were pieces of hollowed-out lead weighing about four ounces that slid onto the manila hemp lead line. Some would become crushed over a season from wear and other banging around. Seated at a special little bench you picked up each one, put it onto an iron peg, pushed down on a handle and re-formed the lead's centre hole so it was ready for stringing on the lead line. There were thousands of them, so it took some time.

Lacing proceeded at a steady pace. Then we came close to the end and the decision had to be made about how to put in a taper on the bunt end. This meant we wanted to make the net shallower, but first a review of what we had. Overall, we were aiming for a three-and-a-half-strip net. This meant three strips of hundred-mesh conventional web and one half strip, that is fifty meshes, of lead line web. These lead line meshes were usually bigger than the body web, six inches as opposed to four inches (fifteen instead of ten centimetres), and made of heavier twine. But the net tapered at the bunt end. The bunt end was where the fish would end up, so bunt web meshes were a bit smaller and made of heavier twine. This was the "moneybag." The taper made the net go from three and a half strips to three strips at the bunt. The question was: how long should the taper be? As I recall it was ten fathoms. Because of the complexity of this decision we delayed cutting the taper until we had hung the cork line and the lead line. We had twenty stretches, or 240

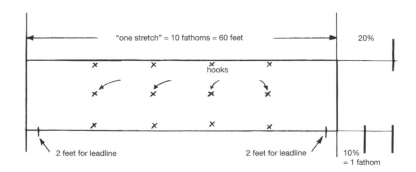

MARKS ON NET LOFT FLOOR
BONES BAY—1953

The marks on the floor of the Bones Bay net loft guided us in making our small three-and-a-half-strip (350-mesh) cotton seine. Seines were made up each year, and there was no book to show us how to do it.

fathoms, of three and a half strips of laced web, plus a little more for shrinkage.

Figuring out that last bit, how much to add for shrinkage, was a big problem for the workers in the net loft. You first built the net at the legal two hundred fathoms but it would shrink when put in the water and then would be stretched a bit from consistent towing. So how much would it shrink and then how much would it stretch? The fear was that if the Fisheries officers measured your net and it was over the legal limit of two hundred fathoms you were fined. Further, you had to go to a port and shorten your net, losing valuable fishing time. Some would put in an extra fifteen fathoms, but we put in seven. Why? There was no clear reason. So we now had 247 fathoms of laced web, with a taper, to be hung on 207 fathoms of cork line.

Now we had to prepare the cork and lead lines in the net loft. These were manila hemp lines and being organic they were subject to rot, wear and shrinkage. They had to be replaced every so often depending upon their condition. Our decision in 1953 was to add about eighty fathoms of new cork line and about forty of lead line. New lines had to be stretched to get out the kinks and eliminate the natural tendency for them to coil up. The objective was to have the purse lines, when fishing, coil and uncoil without kinks. This straightening was achieved by using a little tow motor, a sort of powered cart. The line was tied to the tow motor and was run around several posts. It was then towed several times. This was done until the line did not appear kinky. Then it was stretched by tying down one end and attaching pulleys to the other until it was stretched, but not too much. The idea was to stretch it but not break it. When the lines were ready for the web to be hung in they were tied to horizontal posts near where the marks on the floor were. The lines were cinched up and made tight, pulled to the right length and then were ready for the web to be hung on them.

SEINE NET

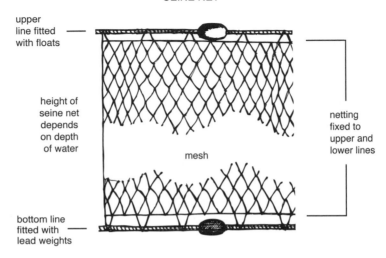

upper
line fitted
with floats

height of
seine net
depends
on depth
of water

netting
fixed to
upper and
lower lines

mesh

bottom line
fitted with
lead weights

The cork line, when ready, was marked at ten fathoms on the floor and strung out tight on two horizontal posts raised above the floor, ready for the web. But as I mentioned, the lead line had to have different marks put on it at two feet on each end of the ten fathoms to make the lead line shorter than the cork line. The overall effect would make the seine have a desired bag. The shorter lead line and the extra web hung in would make the web billow out, hopefully confusing the fish. We never knew what the net actually looked like in the water but through trial and error this design had emerged. Fishermen change things slowly, as mistakes can be costly.

The number of traditional Spanish corks needed was more or less set for the entire net. Perhaps a few extra were added at the bunt end, where the fish ended up. However, the lead line was different. Extra leads were added at the tow end and at the bunt end. This was to ensure the net sunk at the bunt end that would be on the beach. The tow end of the line had a tendency to rise up when extra towing power was added, such as when we were closing the net. Our previous work punching the leads so they would have smooth circular holes was appreciated as they slid smoothly onto the lead line.

Hanging the web proceeded on the same hooks as the lacing of the web but with the corks and leads on their respective lines. Two men hung the cork line while opposite them two others worked on the lead line. Hanging was simple: a knot was made on the line (actually two hitches), and several meshes were picked up by the needle and knotted on the cork line. Two corks were placed in position and another knot was made on the other side of the corks. The same was done for the lead line. And it was all carefully calculated to ensure even distribution of the corks and leads on the two lines. When the ten fathoms was done the lines and web were dropped and pulled to one end, and another stretch was set up, to repeat the procedure. On the wall I placed a mark for each stretch—twenty was the objective, plus the additional seven fathoms, for a 207-fathom net.

During the making of the seine I was able to learn some new skills. Filling needles and punching leads was not difficult. But learning to lace with speed took practice, as did hanging. After picking up a thousand meshes and threading the needle your fingers sure got raw. Learning how the actual net was made was important to me, though, and I paid close attention. But I also graduated to a new task: hanging the becket lines on the lead line. The becket lines were small straps with a metal purse ring in the centre with a clove hitch (two half-hitches). The purse line ran through these rings, closing the net. The ends of the beckets had an eye-splice and were tied to the lead line. I had to learn to make the clove hitch around the purse ring, and learn how to make an eye-splice in three-strand rope. (We never said "rope"; it was always "line.") Finally, a series of hitches with hanging twine tied the beckets to the lead line. These were evenly spaced out. I forget

Hanging a seine. The man on the left has threaded the leads onto the lead line and is hanging the web onto it. His partner is hanging the Spanish corks. GULF OF GEORGIA MUSEUM, CANADIAN FISHING COMPANY COLLECTION 200.050.008

how many rings we tied on, as I later lost the cigarette package on which I wrote it all down. Maybe fifty or sixty.

The taper on the bunt end of the seine was mysterious to me at that time, though later I learned how to do it. It required cutting the web from one edge to another at an angle. The precise angle was about thirty degrees and there was much discussion of how many meshes to cut along and how many to cut up to get the right angle. In any event, it was done. The two strips of bunt were laced to the ordinary body web and the fifty-mesh lead line web was laced to them. The result was two and a half strips on the bunt end, heavily weighted with the extra leads we put on.

Lastly, the ends of the net received a "gable." The vertical end of the net, between the cork line and the lead line, was hung onto another line with small rings attached to it, and a small line was run through the rings. This allowed the gable end to be pursed up, creating a bag in the bunt end. The tow line end of the net also had a gable that could be pursed up. Because the nets were light, this could be done by hand, assuming you were strong. If you weren't, you were not on the boat.

After three or four days, the net was made. But we also had to prepare the purse lines. They were made of four-strand, long-lay manila hemp (the lead and cork lines were three-strand) and required some intricate splicing. The end of each purse line had to

These men are hanging gillnets using special stools with measuring pegs for setting web hanging spaces on the lead line and cork line. Note the black cedar "corks." CITY OF VANCOUVER ARCHIVES CVA 783-175

have an oval ring in it. This was for a curious joining link called a "figure eight" that linked the two rings spliced into the purse lines, which allowed the purse line to be separated or joined as the case may be. And the splice had to be smooth to allow the purse line to go through the purse rings with ease. The new purse line was unwound from its bale, about three feet of line was selected and the splicing began. Technically it was a back-splice. Once two "tucks" were made—that is, the strands were inserted into the line twice—the strands were trimmed a little and another tuck made. The strands were thinned again and a final tuck made. The end of the purse line now had the ring firmly embedded in it and the splice was tapered to allow easy passage through the purse rings. We repeated the process several times, as there were two purse lines and a shorter lifter line. The lifter received the most wear so it was smaller, about twenty fathoms, and it would be replaced once or twice during the season.

The purpose of the rings on the ends of the purse lines was to allow the lines to be connected through the ingenious metal connector: the figure eight. It looked like a figure eight, hence the name, and it opened up to allow the two rings on each end of the two lines to be inserted and then closed, connecting the two lines. Sounds easy but it was always a tricky manoeuvre to hold the open figure eight in one hand and insert the two purse line links into its open jaws. Done right the figure eight closed up and the two lines were joined. It is seldom used, if at all, now.

There were still a few other tasks to be done. Beach lines had to be made up and perhaps the brailer's meshes had to be mended. The brailer was a scoop, made of web hung on a circular ring about three feet across on a long wooden handle, that dipped the fish out of the net. Easy tasks, but necessary ones. And dealing with the various poles for pushing the net way from the boat, as well as the plungers, which were poles with small boxes on the end, or a piece of pipe on a line. These were to scare fish with and had to be made ready. But the net was done. Now we had to get it onto the *Jean W*, which took some time, as we had to do it by hand. A door on the net loft opened and we pulled the seine outside, over a roller placed on the dock and onto the boat. We now had a conventional three-and-a-half-strip net ready to fish Nimpkish sockeye and whatever else we could get during the season.

The full preparation had taken five days and several cans of corned beef. We left Bones Bay and had a pleasant trip up Clio Channel, into the Johnstone Straits and home to Alert Bay. I now knew how to make a net. Using it was another matter. That was to come.

## CHAPTER THREE

# FISHING NIMPKISH SOCKEYE

In 1953 I joined the small fishing vessel *Jean W* as one of the skiff men. The captain was Arnie Wasden. The *Jean W* was a small seiner built in Alert Bay in 1926, originally to transport the inspector of boilers around to the various logging camps that used steam-powered donkeys. Later the boat was converted to a table seiner and had its heavy-duty Atlas engine removed and a new Gardner diesel one put in.

Table seining was a technique developed to efficiently set the net and get it back aboard. The net was stowed on a box-like turntable mounted on rollers on the stern. This set-up allowed the net to be set directly off the stern. To bring the net aboard the table was turned ninety degrees to face the pursed-up net that was amidships because of the pursing operation. On the end of the table, facing the net, was a powered roller operated by gears under the table. Once the net was aboard the table was turned back to its old position, ready for the next set of the net. This was the standard method of seining until the advent of the Puretic power block in the late 1950s.

It's important to understand how we went about setting the net. To start off, the boat pulled up as close as possible to the beach at the setting spot, and at a command of "Let 'er go!" the skiff's painter (towing line) was untied and the skiff cut loose. On the outward side of the skiff was a slip knot hitch with the beach line connected to it. The other end of that line was connected to the end of the net. Once the skiff was launched, the skiff man dug in one oar and the effect of the hitch was to turn the skiff sideways and point it to the shore, and at the same time pull the seine net off the table. Pulling the slip knot released the skiff from the beach line. Nowadays a small sea anchor is used to pull the net off the drum.

The beach man retrieved the skiff's painter and then leapt ashore with the beach line. The beach line had one purpose: to hold the net to the shore against the tide. The beach man then tied it to a tree, a rock, a peg or whatever was available. (Over time, safe setting spots had been discovered and these acquired their own descriptive names.) Meantime, the crew on the boat set the net in a small arc and started towing. The purse lines were coiled on deck and as the net was set they ran out through the purse rings on the side of the table. Sometimes, to ensure no purse line hang-ups, the lines were run over a pole held off the deck. Coiling the purse lines neatly was essential to avoid snarls, which would cause all sorts of problems on deck—chief amongst them was that a line getting caught up would stop the setting of the net.

The boat usually towed the net for twenty minutes. Where this convention came from I don't know. At the end of that time, the bow of the boat was pointing to the beach and when it got close the skipper signalled to the beach man to let go, meaning he should untie the beach line. Holding the end of the beach line, the beach man would get back into the skiff and the skiff man would row them out to the boat. The beach man handed the beach line to someone on deck, who put it through a pulley block in a davit

Crewmen bringing aboard the net, on the table at the boat's stern. The purse rings are on the side of the net table with the purse line threaded through them. CITY OF VANCOUVER ARCHIVES PHOTOGRAPH #CVA 586-921

and onto the winch. This procedure closed the net, but it was not yet pursed up. Once the end of net was up to the davit, the beach line was disconnected from that curious metal gadget called a "blondie" (which is still in use). Its purpose was to connect the beach line to the purse line by use of a figure eight, and to hold that link immobile in the blondie, which stopped the pulling of the purse line while the beach line was holding the net to the shore. Once the blondie was released the beach line pulled on the purse line and pursing began.

Both ends of the net were pursed. The purse lines ran through two davits on the side of the boat and two large, and very neat, coils were made on the deck as they were pulled in. While two men were pursing the skiff man and the cork line man on the stern were busy. The pursing of the net drew the boat into the middle of the net. When it was pursed up, many of the corks on the cork line were around the stern and the bow. On the *Jean W* the corks were piled by me on the stern and the skiff man piled his onto the skiff and then later pushed his around to the side of the boat where we would bring the net up. I also pushed my corks off the table and used a pole to push them around to the side of the boat.

Now it was time to get the rest of the net aboard. The table had been turned and the crew now took their positions to haul the net back in. It took five men: one man was on the cork line, three men each had a strip of web (one hundred meshes) and one man was on the lead line. The lead line man was pulling the line off the deck and piling it on the table. The cork line man had to pile the corks in a somewhat artistic manner. In those days it was a matter of pride to have a "nice looking pile." The real purpose was to ensure the corks came off the table in a smooth way next time. The five men worked in unison to bring the seine back aboard. It was brought aboard evenly, so each man had to keep up; you had to pull your section of the net, and the man on the other side of you made sure of that.

Once the bunt was reached the men left the table and went on deck to "dry up." This meant pulling up the loose web in the "bunt"—the bag that had the fish—and getting ready to bring the fish aboard. If there were a lot of fish a brailer was used. This large dip net with a pursed bottom would be released when it was over the hatch. A brailer held about one hundred large salmon. When the brailing was done the rest of the net, the bunt, was pulled onto the table.

Arrangements were then made for the next set. First, the purse line needed to be passed through the rings on the net and hooked up to the blondie. The beach line was also put in the blondie. The table was turned and the net was ready. We pulled the skiff up to the stern and tied its painter. At that point we always did a curious thing: we took a piece of twine and tied the

This 1947 image from the lower Johnstone Straits shows the crew of one boat brailing fish and the crew of another pulling in their seine over a powered roller on the net table. COURTESY ALAN HAIG-BROWN

The brailer, a large dip net, was used to scoop the fish out of the net and release them into the hatch. Fish pumps were later used in the herring and sardine fisheries. HARBOUR PUBLISHING ARCHIVES

last purse ring to some coiled purse line. The objective was to make sure that an extra part of the purse line came off with the net. The purpose of this extra slack was to ensure a tight purse line didn't bunch up the net. It was, to my mind, only a symbolic precaution. Anyway, when pursing started the twine broke, freeing the purse line. Previously, we had pulled about four fathoms of purse line through the rings and piled it on the stern on the gable end to provide this purse line slack.

Setting the net took about five minutes, towing was about twenty and pursing was about fifteen minutes. Hauling the net took about twenty minutes, making it about one hour altogether for a set. The time varied when you were fishing pink salmon in the inlets, though: longer tows were made, as the fish were less active. In the Johnstone Straits, with the strong tides there, shorter tows of twenty minutes were the norm. The flood tide lasted about six hours so it was normal to make four or five sets on the flood and then perhaps look for a spot where the fish were found in the ebb. Fishing the Nimpkish River there was no ebb tide set. However, the rule of thumb in the Straits was to fish Blinkhorn Island on the flood, then go around Hanson Island to Double Bay and fish the ebb there. Rarely did we make ten sets; six or seven was considered enough, seeing as it was all manual labour.

Certain skills were necessary for a successful operation. The skiff man had to be able to row; this was done standing up, and often the skiff had to be manoeuvred in rough water. The beach man had to know the tie-ups and always get the beach line secured to a good tree or rock. The men on deck, usually the cook and the engineer, had to coil the purse lines expertly and know how to splice lines, plus mend holes in the net. This was in addition to their duties of cooking and looking after the engine (which mainly required making sure the generator was charging the batteries for the electricity on the boat). Of course, the most important man was the skipper and he had to know a lot. How the tide acted and how the fish acted and where the good setting spots were and a myriad of other things. To a degree, some of it was a case of "monkey see, monkey do." That is, you merely had to follow successful boats and copy their moves.

There were a host of other minor skills to know as a fisherman: how to mend holes in the net in addition to lacing and hanging, how to splice lines and make lashings, and how to use the troublesome figure eights to connect the links in lines. Then there were the unwritten codes of behaviour. There was only one

The FV *W-11*, one of the BC Packers fleet of "W-numbered" boats, about 1950. In those days they didn't use a sea anchor to pull the net off the table. The skiff man is ready to go. CITY OF RICHMOND ARCHIVES PHOTOGRAPH #1985-6-1462

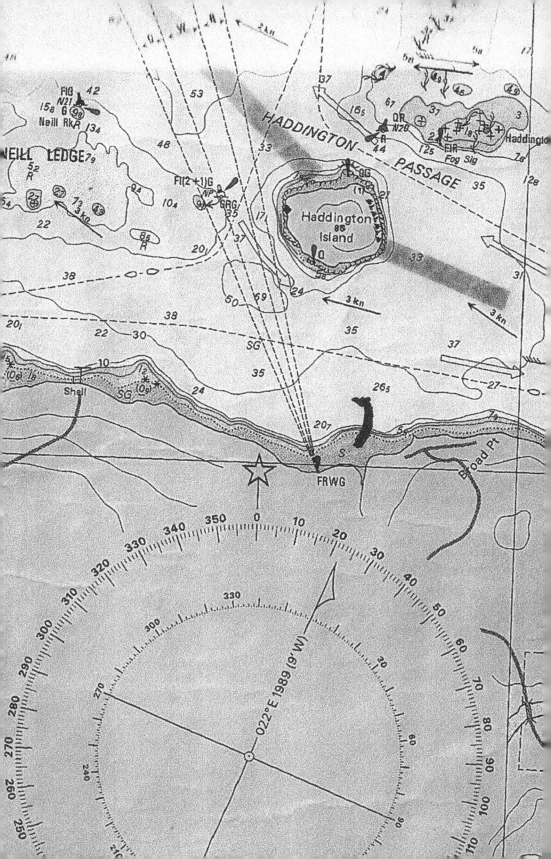

26

27     30     33     29

26

31                                    35

15₂

14₆                                            C O

162    7₃   3  Leonard Rk                        33
              26                      35

46                                            3

35                      31          14₆    S
                                                    S     2₅
                 24                                        SG    0₆

26                              20₁

33                                   (0₆)
                                                IR
31                                        120        CORMORAN

20₁        20₁                 (0₉)                      18₁
                                                              DR
                              16₉              F I W R        FR
27                                              SG  R
                          24          31              (4)    Alert Bay    7₀
28              82    2₈        FIG                              11
                              N17      27              R     S           8₂
     27                  Alert Rk  0₆          30          37                143
              20₁            Kish R     V₅    (96)  GSh                          R
                          (0₉)  (14)      20₁              33    3 kn
                                                      10              2₅
                  85      2₁        15    3₇  10          5₂      Inset/Cartouche    3 kn  22
                              2₁  12                                          R
                    16₅      2₁  (11)  0₉  (2₄)          6        17₁
NIMPKISH RIVER  Flagstaff lt    (11)  2₄  4₆  Nimpkish Bk              G
     SG        15                  4₃  18  18  0₃  7₃              24
                    0₉              0₆  0₃  2        4₃
IR                          1₂  0₃  0₆  8          7₃  14₆
                                                    18  3₇
                          Ru    SG      0₃  1₂  18      15₅
                    Ru              0₉          2₁
     19      Thiemer          (1)                              4₃

place on the boat that was your own, and it was your bunk. All other space was more or less common property. That meant you could not leave an oilskin, jacket or magazine unattended. Also, you had to be respectful of other people's space. The emphasis was on cooperation and conflict was avoided. And the superstitions you had to abide by were many. One that was unique to salmon fishermen was the horror of opening a can upside down. If it happened, the label was immediately ripped off. In some ways, when I started out in 1953 it seemed like learning the ins and outs of life on board was just as crucial as learning how to set and pull in the net.

My first experience seining, then, was that summer of 1953 aboard the *Jean W.* In addition to our seine, we would have four-strand purse lines, a small brailer, fish peoghs, little poles for pushing the net away from the boat and plungers for scaring fish. The skiff was about fourteen feet (over four metres) long and came equipped with two oars and a beach line for tying the net to the beach. The beach line was my area of business. Soon, I mastered the setting technique. As I mentioned, when the skiff was launched the skiff man rowed me to the shore, then I leapt out and ran up the beach with the line and wrapped it around a tree or rock. I could then survey the set and the world around me.

One bright late May Monday morning we made our first set. We had anchored up the night before at Hyde Creek, as the tide was against us at night. We only set on the flood. At Hyde Creek you set at low water slack and let the first of the flood bring the fish, which were Nimpkish sockeye. A quick inspection of the

PREVIOUS PAGE: This chart shows the three Nimpkish sockeye sets we did in 1953 on the *Jean W.* They were at Hyde Creek, Egg's Place and Dago Bay. REPRODUCED WITH THE PERMISSION OF THE CANADIAN HYDROGRAPHIC SERVICE. NOT TO BE USED FOR NAVIGATION.

kelp to ensure the tide was flooding was necessary. The fronds of the kelp on the surface of the water were a sure indicator of the tide. The tide was never too strong at Hyde Creek so there was a margin for error, and there were also a few snags you could rip your net on. Table seining had its own procedures and it mainly involved muscle power. That is why young, strong boys like me were needed.

After I returned from the shore I handed the end of the beach line to one of the crew at the bow. On the *Jean W* this was the cook. Once the net was at the winch he released the catch on the blondie that allowed the winch to purse the net.

Now the pursing began. Two men piled the purse lines in large coils on the deck, always coiled clockwise (or as we said, "right-handed"). Soon the lifter line was reached, which was always a good-quality line (usually newer purse line) as it had to lift the heavy lead line out of the water. Once it was out of the

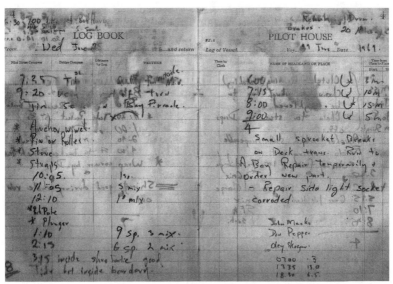

One logbook entry for the *BC Maid* in 1969 chronicles the tide, the sets, the machinery breakdowns and the crew. This early, detailed approach to keeping records was a key to later success. DON PEPPER

water the winch was stopped and dogged to prevent it rolling back. Now two small pieces of canvas were wrapped around the two purse lines and then small chains wrapped around them. Then the chains were put on the "hook," a double fall-block. The double-fall line was put on the winch and the lead line was slowly lifted out of the water. Before it was dropped on deck the leads were split—pushed out—so that when they were dropped on deck they lay on top of each other in an orderly fashion. This was necessary because they had to be pulled by hand off the deck and piled on the net table.

Once the net was pursed up, the lead line was lifted onto the deck and the net table was turned to face the net, the power roller started. It was mounted on the end of the net table and made pulling the net aboard easier. Five of us then pulled the net over the power roller and brought the net back aboard, piling it on the table at the stern of the boat. I had the cork line, and it took some skill to stack the corks so they would go off the table smoothly on the next set.

Five or six sets a day was the norm in those days; I think twice in that season we made ten sets and were exhausted. The relative inefficiency of the technique had a side benefit, though, in that skippers thought carefully about making a set and with five-day openings (six p.m. Sunday to six p.m. Friday) there was time to consider their fishing strategy. Knowledge, skill, luck, determination and hard work all played their part. Good skippers got good boats and had good crews and so it went. As a lowly beach man on a small boat I watched with envy the larger boats and the successful crews. I knew them all, as the Nimpkish was fished almost exclusively by Alert Bay boats. Most of the fishermen were Natives. My skipper was related to a large Native family that had several seiners fishing alongside us, so we had friends to help us in a jam.

Depending on the number of boats lined up to fish we made two or three sets when our turn came at Hyde Creek, and at about half flood we would move to Egg's Place about a mile (a kilometre and a half) away. The place got its name from a man who had a chicken farm there and rowed his eggs to nearby Sointula and Alert Bay for sale. The tide was a little stronger there so I had to tie up the net as fast as possible, running up the beach in my clumsy gumboots and searching frantically for a suitable tree or rock. The key was to not let the end of the net drift out from the shore as the sockeye travelled close to the beach, or so everyone believed.

There was a further problem: black bears hanging out near the shore. On several occasions I had to shout and throw rocks to get the bears away from my tie-up tree. This brought great laughter from the boats watching me. Why the bears liked that spot I don't know. Whenever we set our net there everyone would hoot and holler at me to watch out for bears. For some reason the fishing was better at Egg's Place than at Hyde Creek. But the truth is we never got very many fish. I think we fished because we had nothing else to do, we were fishermen. Also it was the captain's way of breaking in the crew. I was seventeen years old, and the skiff man was fifteen. Late in the next season on the *Jean W*, I was the oldest of four boys at eighteen, with my brother at seventeen and two other brothers, the owners' sons, at seventeen and sixteen.

The third setting spot was known as "Dago Bay" back in those racially insensitive times; the nickname arose because some Italian fishermen liked to fish there in the 1930s and 1940s. The bay was at the mouth of the Nimpkish River, and you set your net at high water slack or close to it because the bay was very shallow, your net was on the bottom in several places and the fishing area was very small, just big enough to set your net in. The place was good for only one set, as the tide soon turned bad—the ebb tide could push your net onto rocks. Not good. After high water we went back to Hyde Creek and anchored up for several hours until the tide was flooding again. Sometimes we even went home to Alert Bay and tied up at the BA Oil dock in the village.

I only fished the Nimpkish for two seasons, 1953 and 1954, on the *Jean W*. After that I was a full-fledged fisherman and could move up to a better boat. But as the *Jean W* was my first, the memories of those two seasons are vivid and clear. Did we make any money? Well, you could say that's all relative. My take-home crew share in 1953 was $1,490. I fished from June 10 to September 15. So I made about $100 per week over the fifteen weeks of fishing from Sunday at six p.m. to Thursday or Friday at six p.m. That amount does not include weekend work on the net. To put it in perspective, my earnings were enough to pay for my first year of university in Vancouver. (Room and board was $40 per month.) It certainly was hard work. And it certainly was different.

Table seining lasted for another four or five years and then the boats switched to the Puretic power block, a technique still being use in many fisheries of the world. Those of us who pulled by hand with the power roller were part of a world now long passed by. As were the Nimpkish sockeye, which were almost wiped out in 1957 by the spraying of DDT on the forests to combat insects. I actually watched the spraying by the planes while working at the Merry Widow mine near Port McNeill.

No one fishes Nimpkish sockeye anymore. Like many small fisheries on the coast it has disappeared. But I will always remember that fishery, as it introduced me to the world of fishing. That's where I paid my dues.

# CHAPTER FOUR

# FISHING DOUBLE BAY AND BLINKHORN

Every fisherman has a strong memory of their first big set or big haul. That moment can be recalled in an instant. Mine was over sixty years ago and the details are as clear now as they were then—and perhaps clearer. I was fishing on the small salmon seiner the *Jean W* and we had fished for Nimpkish sockeye in late June of 1953 and it was time to move to the traditional Alert Bay fishing grounds around Double Bay and Blinkhorn, two fishing areas where tide was important. The two places were closely linked, as one was good on the flood tide, the other on the ebb. On a typical day you set your net on each tide at least once and, depending on the strength of the ebb or flood tide, maybe twice or more. This two-tide approach allowed the skipper to plan a day's fishing.

The salmon moved according to the tides and their behaviour was varied, but certain overall patterns were evident to the observant fisherman. On the ebb tide they came into Double Bay and on the flood tide they were to be found at Blinkhorn (technically Blinkhorn Island, on the charts). At each place there were select fishing spots and tie-ups.

To understand our fishing strategy, you have to know how the tides worked. In the Johnstone Straits the tides had a somewhat well-defined pattern. The flood and the ebb tides were each about six hours long (not quite) and they varied in their strength, depending on the phase of the moon. The tides got bigger each day until they peaked and then got smaller each day until the cycle was repeated. The size of the tide affected the currents in the Straits and they affected the fish. A big tide pushed the salmon farther south during the flood, a small tide not so much. A big ebb tide would sometimes force the salmon back. Knowing the tide and how it affected the currents was necessary to gauge what the fish were up to. Also, different tides affected different fishing spots. For example, a large flood would push salmon out of Baronet Pass on Cracroft Island, across the Straits and back, north, into Bauza Cove, above Blinkhorn. Otherwise, the salmon would usually go in a southerly direction when they were in the Straits and not go into Bauza Cove at all. Blinkhorn was some sort of cut-off point. Fish were sometimes in Bauza Cove on big tides, but they were always at Blinkhorn.

The timing of the fish was also influenced by the size of the tides. For example, they did not come to Blinkhorn until later in the flood tide, sometimes not until almost high water. The current also determined how the fish acted. On a big flood they were considered "wild," as they seemed to be in hurry. All such factors had to be considered by the skipper if he wanted to understand what was happening with the fish.

Like Blinkhorn, when it came to setting the net at Double Bay there were the usual unwritten rules that had to be followed. The rules revolved mainly around the taking of turns. The first boat at a spot was the leader, and the setting order was established as each new boat arrived. The second boat would call the first to confirm their turn was next, the third boat would call the second boat and so on. A new arrival at the spot merely asked "Who's last?" and then got his turn from that boat. Certain other rules applied, too. Once a boat had set his net he was allowed more or less twenty minutes to tow before starting to close it up. While closing it he might tell the next boat it was okay to set, otherwise the next boat could be guilty of "shutting him off" (setting a net in front of his net), which was a breach of protocol. These rules were rough and ready but seemed to be acceptable to all.

Here is how it all worked on that day in late July of 1953, according to my records—a messy page in a schoolboy scribbler I have kept all these years. We had anchored up the day before in Double Bay. We were up before daylight. We had the usual toast and coffee, although I actually drank tea. I checked the skiff, and the oars were tied down and the beach line was neatly coiled. I put on my oilskins and a warm jacket. We left the harbour and were soon at our setting spot, just off "the Double Bay Rock," and found our turn. We were third, after the *Cape Ross*. I watched that boat's set. It had to be done in a special way, as it was a tricky spot and you could rip your net easily. The end of the net was dropped some distance offshore from the tie-up as the bottom was "itchy" (meaning it was foul ground) and two beach lines were necessary. Beach men hated running two lines, as you had to hook them up with that special connector called a figure eight. It was sometimes a difficult thing for me to do as a greenhorn.

After closing his net the skipper of the *Cape Ross* said "Go ahead," and we set our net. I landed on the rock and wrapped the beach line around the post that was there. I could now examine the set. The seine went straight out rather than in the usual arc,

Following page: Alert Bay fishermen traditionally set at Blinkhorn on the flood tide and in Double Bay on the ebb tide. REPRODUCED WITH THE PERMISSION OF THE CANADIAN HYDROGRAPHIC SERVICE. NOT TO BE USED FOR NAVIGATION.

again because of the bad bottom. There was just a small hook in the shape of the net at the outer end. We were fishing pink salmon, so I looked for jumpers coming into our net. I could see them jumping and I kept shouting "Coming in!" which is what beach men were supposed to do to let the skipper know there were fish coming, assuming he may not see them. In this case, they just kept coming.

The *Jean W* slowly turned and headed for the beach, towing the net around to form a long ellipse, which is how you set off the Rock. At the skipper's signal I untied the beach line and jumped into the waiting skiff. We rowed out to the boat and I handed the end of the beach line to the man on the bow and he took it along the boat and put it into the davit and then on the winch, and slowly winched the beach end over to the boat. Once the end was hooked up, he released the blondie that held the beach line and the purse line, preventing pursing until it was released. This was the usual procedure. We now were pursing both ends of the net. I moved onto the seine table and started pulling on the cork line to bunch the corks on the table. As we pursed the boat moved into the net so it was necessary to stop the corks from going around behind the boat. Once the net was pursed up I used a pole to push the pile of corks off the table and into the net, so that all of the net was in front of itself—that is, all on one side of the boat, ready to be hauled in. The skiff man was up on deck by this time as well and doing the same at his end.

We did the usual tasks. The lead line was hoisted on deck and the purse line removed from the rings attached to the lead line. We could now start bringing the net back aboard. But we were excited: we had *lots* of fish and they were bubbling in the net. Lots of bubbles, lots of fish. We knew we had a good set, so we pulled with a light heart. When we reached the end, the bunt, we got off the table and went to the rail and dried up the bunt. We could feel the weight of the fish. Once we were dried up we were ready to brail the fish into our hold.

By modern standards it was a small set but it was my first big one, netting over 3,500 pink salmon. The brailer's pole allowed you to shove the brailer deep into the net full of fish and scoop them up. The winch then lifted the brailer out of the net and it was swung over the hatch, where the drawstring at the bottom of the brailer was released so the fish fell into the hatch. Our method was for the skipper to be in the skiff, to which the cork line was attached. He would guide the brailer. I was on the pole and shoved it as deep as I could. The winch man lifted it out and one of the crew guided the brailer over the hatch. One crewman controlled the drawstring on the brailer and he was unfortunately called the "asshole" man. We were a green crew, kids actually, and not very good at brailing, but we got the job done.

In the evening we went into Double Bay to the packer. We pitched our fish out of the hold and onto our deck and then onto the company packer. It was hard work with fish peoghs (our single-tined pitchforks). We finished about midnight. I went to my bunk very tired but happy. After our big set we had that indefinable confidence so necessary to being a good fisherman.

We fished the Blinkhorn–Double Bay circuit many times, going around Hanson Island either through Baronet Pass or through the "blowhole" (a tricky entrance to Double Bay not for the fainthearted) on the other end of Hanson. It all depended upon the tide. We did venture farther sometimes as well, going into the Mainland Inlets (the Broughton Archipelago). I liked fishing there as the sets had long tows and I could relax on the beach and watch the slow-moving humps go into our net. But the catches there were small and we would long for the big hauls that could be made in Double Bay and the Johnstone Straits.

Around that time, I was still getting an education in being a fisherman. As the beach man I had the opportunity to look at each set and assess its potential for catching fish. This easily and naturally led me to evaluate the skipper, although I never said anything to him. It was just not done. His word was law and I was just seventeen. In addition to learning the skills I came to adopt the philosophy of the fisherman: perennial optimism. If you had a bad haul, in effect failure, well, there was always the next set.

Disappointment came with the job, but so did success. Fishermen are dreamers and optimists but also hard realists. A positive attitude was a powerful antidote to rainy days, hunger and fatigue, lack of fish and cramped quarters. You learned to conquer envy. There was always a boat that caught more fish than yours, and you had to be able to live with that. I was fishing with a greenhorn skipper on a small boat and had to watch Louie Benedet on the FV *Ermelina* brail aboard eight thousand humps early one morning from his set in Baronet Pass, while we had a measly two hundred fish aboard. Part of my education was to learn from Louie's skill but also to have the ability to handle envy and place it in context. Louie pioneered that special set, which is known as "The Bank," as like a bank it is only open a few hours a day on the tide. Why? It is a scary place to fish with very strong tides, and not for the timid or those with bad gear.

I fished one more year on the *Jean W*. In 1954 there were no fish in the Straits so we went to the Gulf of Georgia and tried to catch Adams River sockeye with our little three-and-a-half-strip net. We were pitiful compared to the big double-decker seine boats with their eight-strip nets. They normally fished the Blue Line in Juan de Fuca Strait but they were also allowed into the gulf. We caught six hundred fish, they caught thousands.

Nonetheless, the *Jean W* was good to me. It was my apprentice-ship. I knew how to fish Nimpkish sockeye, at Double Bay and Blinkhorn and many other places. It was time to become a jour-neyman. I was ready.

## CHAPTER FIVE

# FO'C'SLE LIFE

**W**ent I first went aboard the *Jean W* in 1953 my mother outfitted me. She gave me a cotton sheet, a woollen blanket and a handmade comforter. A small pillow was added. She also put a towel, a spare pair of woollen socks and a book in the pillowcase. I was dressed as a fisherman. I had a Stanfield's undershirt, a woollen shirt overtop it and a warm coat. For fishing I had a lovely (to me) pair of hip gumboots and a sou'wester rain hat. I had no extra clothes. Being the tallest member of the crew at six feet three inches I chose the longest bunk in the fo'c'sle, which was the crew's quarters. I recall it perfectly—it was the lower portside bunk.

The owner of the *Jean W* was also the cook, and his son-in-law was the skipper. The owner was over seventy years old and usually grouchy. In no uncertain terms he told me that I was to leave nothing of mine in the galley, or he would throw it overboard. I was soon to learn fish boat etiquette. The only space you could call your own was your bunk. You could not touch anything on another person's bunk. All other space was communal. The crew slept in the fo'c'sle, and the skipper and cook had their bunks on the main deck. The fo'c'sle was incredibly small; in the morning only one person could dress at a time. You got up, opened the little door and went through the engine room (a lovely Gardner diesel) and up the ladder into the galley, where you said good morning to the cook. He had coffee and toast ready. We would mostly sit in silence, while contemplating the day ahead. It was not yet daylight.

Soon it was time to pull the anchor and get ready for fishing. Usually we had only a short run to the setting spots. After a month of fishing my hands had toughened up so that they no longer burned in the morning and my fingers were not claw like. Pulling on lines and the net meant your hands became calloused. The story was that you were supposed to urinate on your hands in the morning to soften them up. I never did. After the first set of the net we had breakfast. Bacon or ham and eggs and maybe fried potatoes. When finished you formally thanked the cook for the meal. Back out on deck you were supposed to help the skipper look for fish but being the beach man I could get into the skiff, on the pretext that I had to be ready when we set the net, but I could then sleep a bit.

During the day us crewmen were supposedly always ready to set the net. But we grabbed catnaps whenever we could. Lunch was usually soup and sandwiches between sets, eaten hurriedly on many occasions. At the end of the day when we were anchored up I washed my hands and face in a small enamel washbasin, then went below. I undressed and got into my bunk. One of the problems of sleeping in a confined space was that you were surrounded by your fellow crewmen. The hard physical labour seemed to promote snoring. Worse were the teeth grinders and even worse were those subject to nightmares. On occasion, some became sleepwalkers. I was never prone to these problems but my brother was a snorer.

On the *Jean W* I learned the unspoken rules of fo'c'sle life and how you functioned in narrow spaces on a fish boat at sea. The emphasis was on suppressing your personal demands for the greater good, more fish. Sometimes angry words were exchanged but the prevailing attitude was one of cooperation. This, of course, often resulted in crew members keeping their thoughts to themselves, often leading them to becoming non-communicative. All over some perceived slight or injustice. You soon sensed this in a shipmate and wisely respected it. In times of great tension, conversation amongst us became mainly monosyllables related to the work at hand. Such was life on small boats.

The pattern set on the *Jean W* was mine for many years. Aboard the small seiners I fished on you slept in the fo'c'sle. The toilet had a door but you used a bucket of sea water to flush. You were always conscious of other people. We crewmen could escape from the skipper's or cook's watchful eyes by going into the skiff or sleeping on the net. We were always tired. There was something indefinable about being a good shipmate. The tasks were straightforward but living and working in a small space required an attitude that focused on cooperation. Having the ability to accept disappointments was also a large part of survival. The rewards were always uncertain. However, I did make a living from fishing. To my mind I was making good, if not big, money.

It was not all work and no play, though. Being young we sometimes played childish pranks on one another. If you fell asleep on the net someone might tie your leg to a cleat and then wake you abruptly to see you tumble. Or you could put several inches of water in someone's gumboots. Stitching up one leg of a fellow crewman's pants was another favourite. I made a small sling and soon became adept at slinging potatoes at other fish boats. If you had a powerful deck hose it was ideal for spraying other boats as you went past. But these were random occurrences. The hard physical labour took its toll on us. If there was any slack time we usually just wanted to sleep.

I moved out of the fo'c'sle when I went to fish reduction herring on the FV *Vanisle* in 1963. The boat was a large "double-decker" that had the crew's accommodation on the main deck. What comfort! I had a large bunk, a locker for my spare clothes and a small drawer under the bunk for my personal things. It was so spacious there was room for everything personal I brought along. The fishing was much easier also, as we used the power block to handle our large seine. We were never as physically tired as when we were fishing salmon. The fishing was relaxed, cruising for hours looking for herring. When we had a load of herring, one hundred tons, we had a ten-hour trip to the reduction plant at Namu and a ten-hour trip back. Wheel turns (steering the boat) for two men were four hours long and with an eight-man crew you could go for days without a wheel turn. While looking for herring it was mainly the skipper and me at the wheel, so it was only while travelling that wheel turns were set up.

When I returned to fishing in the 1980s (it was sporadic at first, a week-long trip or so), I fished on the first aluminum *Prosperity*. The new *Prosperity* was built in 1990 and I had access to all the modern conveniences: a flush toilet, a shower, a spacious stateroom, a bunk with a reading lamp, a curtain for privacy and a soft mattress. The skipper had his own stateroom in the bow, the cook and engineer had their own two bunk staterooms and the larger stateroom had four bunks. All of the bunks had lockers and drawers for personal effects. So there was no more fo'c'sle living as such. The other change over time was in our clothing. In 1953 I wore what little I had every day and took it home to be washed at the end of each trip. I don't think I had a complete change of clothes on board. However, I did have spare woollen socks as I always seemed to get my feet wet. Keeping warm and dry was a priority. Woollen shirts and pants helped. Fishermen sometimes wore a special kind of pants called "bannockburns." They were heavy woollen pants mixed black and brown in colour. A belt could be used to hold them up but they were heavy so suspenders (that we called "braces") were used, and were indeed almost necessary. Bannockburns were expensive and hard to find. I never wore them, but those who did were clearly saying that they were serious fishermen.

Rain gear was necessary. In my early days the skipper and the cook could get by with an oilskin apron of the sort worn by fish plant workers but us crewmen needed something more substantial. Some wore black rubber Miner raincoats but they were too heavy and uncomfortable for me. Most of us had rain pants and

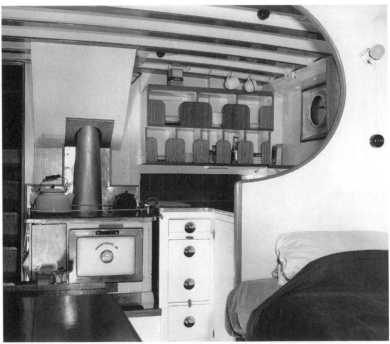

In the small galleys of the early seiners, pieces of plywood would often be mounted on the shelves to hold the dishes in place. IMAGE NA-09321 COURTESY OF ROYAL BC MUSEUM, BC ARCHIVES

wore a short raincoat over them; they were usually yellow. Finally, some of us wore cheap cotton gloves until our hands became calloused enough.

In later years rain gear improved as new materials were developed, but in the main fishermen's gear looked the same in the 1990s as it did in the 1950s. A few changes were made, though. The power block brought the net down onto the crewmen so some took to wearing the hard hats that were already prevalent in the forestry and construction industries. Sometimes the rain gear left abrasions on your wrists so some wore "wristers," usually short woollen sleeves. The abrasions could cause salt-water boils, which were painful and hard to get rid of.

The work was hard and sometimes rewarding, sometimes not. When I started there was no unemployment insurance, no Workers' Compensation, no pension, just your earnings. Income tax was not deducted so sooner or later fishermen ran afoul of the taxation authorities. I never filed or paid any until I was thirty-four—that's when the taxman finally found me. The big change had to be the better living conditions as the boats got larger and more money was being made.

But no matter how spacious and comfortable the crew accommodations were aboard those later vessels, my early seasons aboard the small seiners really formed who I was as a fisherman. There is something indefinable that happens when you spend many years in the fo'c'sle. You develop an attitude about how you conduct yourself and interact with other people. Being conscious of your shipmates translates into a concern for, or at least an awareness of, how others react to your actions. Further, you

FOLLOWING PAGE: Use of the power block up in the boom meant hard hats were necessary. Among the dangers was the chance of stinging jellyfish landing on those working below. IMAGE I-29318 COURTESY OF ROYAL BC MUSEUM, BC ARCHIVES

get used to and come to expect the little niceties, such as always thanking the cook for a meal, being relatively neat in your personal habits, sharing the work and being sought after as a good shipmate. Such was fo'c'sle life.

## CHAPTER SIX

# FINDING FISH

*That which is far off and exceeding deep, who can find it out?*
— Ecclesiastes 7:24

How do fishermen find the fish? Well, they know where to look. As I mentioned, we Alert Bay fishermen fishing for salmon had a simple formula that was modified over time: fish in the Johnstone Straits on the flood and fish in Double Bay on Hanson Island on the ebb. It worked long ago and it works now. But as fishing became more competitive and there were more and more boats this strategy had to be refined. So we fishermen found niches that satisfied our needs. The Finnish Sointula fishermen remained in one spot, Finn Rock in Double Bay. Other boats were more venturesome, going to the top end of Malcolm Island and fishing the flood to Lizard Point and then doubling back to Malcolm Point on the ebb. In the Straits some boats specialized in fishing the Vancouver Island shore from Blinkhorn down to Fine Beach below Robson Bight, and occasionally fishing Cracroft Island spots such as the Pig Ranch and Boat Harbour. The fishing patterns depended upon fish behaviour, which was generally well known: they were mainly heading south, perhaps to the Fraser River. Obviously, fishermen varied their strategies depending upon the species (sockeye or pinks), the strength of the run and tide and current conditions. But the Blinkhorn–Double Bay pattern was fairly consistent.

Watching for fish was an acquired skill, and some were better at it than others. Keen eyesight was a requirement for finding salmon. They "showed" by jumping. You could see them as they swam along and gave a leap. I always assumed they jumped in order to practise leaping up waterfalls to get to their spawning grounds. In any event, as they moved in the tide they jumped and sometimes "finned," which was just showing their backs above the water. Over time, it became easy to identify schools of salmon and predict their size. While setting the net it was possible to see several large schools enter the net and hear the joyful cries of the beach man as he shouted "Coming in!"

When we fished the Blue Line in Juan de Fuca Strait for salmon we did not look for fish; we had to set when it was our turn in the lineup, regardless. Also, the salmon were travelling deep (we used deep nets, eight and a half strips) and we could not see them, as they didn't jump much. However, they *did* show when they were leaving your net. They would jump in the back quarter of the net on the tow end, so on the *Prosperity* one person was delegated to watch that section. As soon as a fish showed there it was time to close the net as the sockeye were definitely starting to head out of the net. Sockeye were tricky like that (as were dog salmon). Humps were not so tricky, being, in the main, slower moving fish and from our perspective not as wild.

Each species of salmon has its own method of showing. Sockeye, being powerful swimmers, shoot along the top of the water somewhat like surfers. Humps leap into the air with a jump that lifts them out of the water like flying fish. Coho are a little like humps, but seem to jump any old which way. Dog salmon show like sockeye. In my experience they have a special trait, in that they show in the same spots and in the same way year after year. This is of course an exaggeration, but if they show fifty feet (fifteen metres) off the kelp in Big Bay on Hanson Island then they will always show there. Strange but true.

Most of what was said above applied to the Johnstone Straits and the Blue Line at Juan de Fuca. Fishing the Mainland Inlets or in northern areas was different. Sometimes the fish were lethargic once they entered an inlet, other times not. Generally fishermen knew fish behaviour in the areas they fished. Otherwise, why were they there?

Finding and catching salmon was one thing; fishing for herring was another thing entirely. Finding the herring was usually a case of watching for birds. Birds could find herring from their "put up," tiny bubbles of methane gas that showed on the surface of the water, well, from their farts. The problem was determining how many herring were in the school. In the early, early days of herring fishing the technique was to lower a lead "cannonball" on piano wire into the water over the school and then feel the bumps with your fingers on the wire as the wire hit the fish in the school. It was said that some fishermen could predict with accuracy the size of a school using this technique. A nice bit of folklore regardless.

Herring also show on the surface of the water, as "flippers." It was possible to find and catch them by sight alone, but that was not an efficient technique. The arrival of the depth sounder changed that. My first experience using sounders was with the Ekolite paper sounder. It was efficient but somewhat primitive compared to present-day sounders. The sounder sent a signal down into the water and the signal returned and made a black mark on a roll of sounder paper that scrolled out for all to see. Heavy black marks on the paper indicated fish. Some skill, but not much, was needed to estimate the size of the school. A small knob, called the "gain," allowed you to increase the strength of the returned signal so you had to be wary of adjusting it. Too much gain and you were deceiving yourself as to the size and density of the school. This was the standard method of finding fish in the herring reduction fishery until it was closed in the 1960s.

The herring roe fishery that evolved after the closure of the herring reduction fishery had the advantage of better sounders and more importantly sonar. Sonar made finding herring child's play, assuming you could operate all the controls. You were sending out an electronic signal that gave you a 360-degree view that showed up on a screen. But you had to know the tilt angle of the beam and its width and strength (measured in megahertz). Using this information you would estimate the school's size based on the red blotches on the screen. Some sonar operators quickly became expert in using the technique and could not only accurately estimate the size of the school but also understand their movement. In a way, it was not too difficult because the fish were in spawning concentrations and were not travelling anywhere far. Nonetheless, skill was needed in operating the sonar and interpreting the results, as I would learn fishing the Foote Islands.

Seeing and finding fish is one thing. Knowing their behaviour is another. Only long experience and intuition can help you maximize the number of fish you get in a haul. This knowledge is important at the start of a run especially, as it enters the fishing grounds. Two examples come to mind. In 1962, when we had a phenomenal run of pinks in Fitz Hugh Sound, we knew they were coming in what we called the "motherlode." Late Thursday afternoon, our last day of fishing for that week, I was on the *W R Lord* and we made our last set in what was back then called "Jap Bay." The tidal surge from Hakai Pass came across the sound and hit the beach directly where we set our net. Rather than the tow of three hundred pinks we expected, we got over four thousand. And they were unusual: small at only three pounds, unlike the usual four-pounders. The skipper said their size was a sure sign of a very big run. And he was right. The 1962 run stands out as one of the largest pink runs in that area.

How Adams River sockeye act in the Johnstone Straits also gives you a clue as to the future run size. In 1958 Harry Stauffer on the FV *Gospuk* got a thousand sockeye on a Sunday night (August 1) at the Izumi Rock set. Then the sockeye were wild over the next few weeks. The fish went back and forth on the flood and ebb tides and didn't move south much from the Blinkhorn area. After two weeks the fish were ready to move and did so. The main body of the run was then in the lower Straits, around Bear River. In 2010 Harry's son Norman ("Hup"), on the FV *Western Moon*, got a similar set at the same place at the same time of the tide and the fish acted more or less the same way as in 1958. The 2010 sockeye run was also one of the biggest. It appears the fish act differently when the runs are very large. These pieces of information may seem arcane but exist as examples of fishermen finding fish, catching them, observing their behaviour and then having the ability to predict their behaviour in the future.

We had much experience with the behaviour of salmon and herring. But when the sardine fishery started in the 1990s there was no experience to draw upon. Most of the old sardine fishermen had died by then. So the problem came to be: how do we find the sardines? Catching them was not too big a problem as the modern, large drum seiner had all the equipment necessary. So in its early days the sardine fishery was mostly spent trying to figure out where the fish were. At first, bird activity was a good sign of their presence. Later the sardines attracted humpback whales so if you found the whales you found the fish. It seemed every year we developed a new theory on sardine behaviour and every year it was found to be wrong. After a few years we became somewhat experienced and knew how to find them. It was really simple: just keep looking.

As part of gaining an understanding of how different species of fish behave, slowly over time I was to learn the ways that fish are affected by tides and currents. The tide generates the currents, which can be somewhat unusual on the BC coast as tidal variations and geography affect the course and the power of the currents. As salmon migrate to their spawning grounds a "fair tide" is useful to them. In other words, swimming with the tide covers more ground than swimming against the tide. From a fisherman's perspective it is a little more complex than that. As tides get larger the currents get stronger and fish move faster and farther on their way to the spawning grounds. The reverse is true as well: during small tides they may not move much at all. The particular behaviour of salmon under these variable tide and current circumstances affects your fishing success. A fisherman has to understand both the fish and the tide.

A case in point: while fishing chum salmon in Glorious Bay (St. Vincent Bay on the charts) in the lower Johnstone Straits, the strength of the tide determines when—at what stage of the tide—the fish will enter the bay. The rule of thumb is that a big tide will push the fish in to the shore, so a tie-up set is possible. Otherwise, the fish never "hit the beach" so you have to set a ways offshore. The difference is that the offshore set is usually shorter in time and more or less a "round set" (not tying to the beach and just making a circle with the net) whereas the beach set, being a "tow set," is longer because the net is tied to the shore. Fishermen favour tow sets as they produce more fish.

There are other examples. A strong tide will cause a tidal

surge from Hakai Pass and push the fish right across Fitz Hugh Sound into the Koeye River boundary setting spots. No fish will be coming up the sound, so no luck until the surge hits. The same circumstance prevails in the Johnstone Straits. Big tides cause tidal surges out of Baronet and Weynton Passes that push the fish into Bauza Cove above Blinkhorn Light. This current causes the fish to go *back*, meaning north instead of south, against all normal expectations.

In contrast, though, there are places where tides and current matter little. One such place is Parson's Bay in Blackfish Sound. Fishermen call it "The Old Man's Home," because the tide there varies little, remaining constant in one direction, and the current is barely perceptible, perhaps one or two knots. These are ideal conditions for those skippers avoiding risk (and excitement). However, you catch few fish there—mostly spring salmon, never sockeye, and occasionally a few pink salmon. And because the catches were primarily spring salmon, Parson's Bay has been closed to fishing for many years.

Sometimes, but rarely, big winds from storms can affect fish behaviour. This is particularly the case during the late fall when fishermen are targeting chum salmon. A big blow will cause the chums to school up and hole up in back eddies. The trick then is to be prepared when they decide to move.

Fish behaviour is mercurial, and analyzing it fraught with error. Only long experience, skill and large portions of luck can result in good catches. In my opinion the most difficult fish to predict, and so catch, are Nimpkish chums, or dog salmon, which were primarily fished in November by Alert Bay fishermen. Their behaviour was confusing: they more or less circled Cormorant Island, hung out on Haddington Reef and moved into Rough Bay on Malcolm Island, or even went south to Blinkhorn. They were also, as fishermen say, "wild." That is, they moved fast, into your net and out again in a flash. As the runs were sporadic, with fishing openings perhaps once or twice in ten years, few fishermen gained experience fishing them.

Luckily for fishermen, the tides and currents on the BC coast are well studied. Tidal stations, little houses with recording gauges in them, dot the coast. Over time, the gathering of many years of data has allowed the oceanographers some confidence in their tidal predictions, which are published as the tide tables. Many factors are at work in producing these results.

The overall process of making the tide tables is complex. First, all the tide data has to be linked to the phases of the moon. The moon is the foundation of tide prediction, as its behaviour is well known. Next the relationship of the moon to the sun has to be integrated into the analysis (called the "quarter rule," after the four phases of the moon). Third, the tide data has to be linked to the passage of the moon locally, before it can all finally be put into a table. The table the fisherman wants has the locality, date, time and size of tide. The fisherman then goes to the page for his particular area and makes his calculations. By comparing several tides over the coast he can see there are fundamental differences. The tides get bigger the farther north you go and the variations are more pronounced.

The rule of thumb for fishermen is that on this coast we have more or less one tide a day (actually one big one and one very small one) in the south and two tides in the north (both more or less the same size). The illustration on the following page shows the various differences in areas of the coast. The first shows the tide in the Johnstone Straits, the second in the Gulf of Georgia and Juan de Fuca Strait.

From the fisherman's point of view he consults the tide book and notes if tides are big or small and which way the trend is. With big tides that are getting bigger he knows, more or less, that the

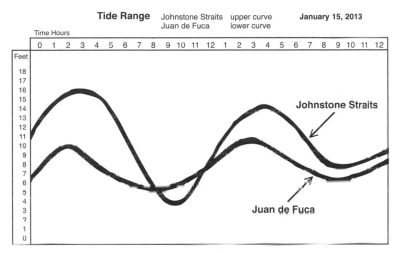

This graph shows the difference in the range of tides. In the Johnstone Straits there was a range of fourteen feet (more than four metres) twice a day, causing strong currents on the flood and the ebb.

salmon will be moving faster and travelling farther. And small tides mean the fish will be slower. This is the case for Johnstone Straits fishermen fishing sockeye, but other areas and species require the same sort of calculation. Fishing the Blue Line (the Bonilla–Tatoosh boundary in Juan de Fuca Strait) requires a calculation of the current's rate during the ebb tide. The ebb tide pushes the net to the fishing boundary. If you go over it you'll be forced to dump your fish, so that danger must enter into your decision of where to set your net. A two-knot ebb means you can set one mile (one and a half kilometres) behind the boundary, tow for thirty minutes and finish up at the boundary line. With modern radar and GPS, not to mention experience, making the calculation is easy.

But the Blue Line had a quirk in its pattern that we exploited many times when I fished on the *Prosperity*. Sooner or later the tide changes the current, from the almost constant westerly current to the east on the flood. This change in current sets up a gyre on Big Bank (La Perouse Bank) and as the flood increases it changes the direction of the current around the gyre. At full flood it has the effect of pushing the fish to the beach on the Blue Line. Once the current is flooding on the beach it is possible to set in close to shore. Normally, fishermen don't set in less than forty-five fathoms on the Blue Line, the rule of thumb (again) being the net fishes at thirty-six fathoms or so (we don't really know). So to be safe, forty-five fathoms of depth is the limit. We once tried fishing in the shallows when the tide was ebbing and lost our net's lead line and a week's fishing. The coral down there just ripped it off. Strangely, you could set on the same spot when the tide was flooding without "hanging up," or snagging your net.

When the tide changed was always our concern there. We used our water temperature gauge to figure that out. When the tide changed and the surge hit the beach, the temperature would leap up a degree or two as warmer surface water came along. We could then leave the long boat lineups on the Blue Line and get several sets in the shallows. Once the fleet saw us setting in the shallows, some boats copied us. No one wanted to be first, though. Setting in the shallows seems like a minor thing but it gave us two or three extra sets. We had often waited up to five hours for our turn on the Blue Line, but in the shallows we set as we wanted. Here is my logbook entry for one typical day:

### Logbook: Blue Line
Monday, August 28, 1989
7:27 – Set in 55 fathoms – 250 fish (number 3 in the lineup)
13:25 – Set in 65 fathoms – 300 fish (long lineup, five-hour wait)
14:28 – Set in 33 fathoms – 600 fish (in the shallows)
15:25 – Set in 30 fathoms – 400 fish (shallows)
17:03 – Set in 33 fathoms – 25 fish (shallows)

We were able to get those three quick sets in the shallows on the flood surge.

Finally, the rate of the current flow varies. Just after slack water the rate changes very quickly and reaches a maximum speed for about one-fifth of the duration of the flow (a little more than an hour). The average rate is about two-thirds of the maximum. So much to know, so little time. Actually, once you committed to fishing a certain place there was a certain cycle to it all. You fished as long as the tide was good and fish were coming. No calculations were necessary, you just kept fishing. But knowing the behaviour of the tide and the resulting currents gave you inner peace and joy as you knew what was in store.

In the early days of fishing I learned much about tides and fish. First, the time spent on the fishing grounds was lengthy. From Sunday at six p.m. to Thursday at six p.m. for the entire opening was the norm. If there were no fish in your area you could move overnight, say a hundred miles, and try new grounds. Second, because the nets were small, pulled by hand and made of cotton, the fishermen took great care in making sets. Perhaps three or four sets on a flood tide and one or two more later on, either on the ebb or the new flood coming seven hours (more or less) later. It is fair to say that six sets were made on an average day on a table seiner with a powered roller, ten sets a day on a Puretic power block seiner and perhaps up to sixteen sets on a modern drum seiner.

Here is the fundamental difference between the boats. On a table seiner, you had the time to master the currents and fish behaviour, and it was a necessity. The Puretic power block reduced that need and made fishing more efficient, allowing more sets and reducing the cost (in time and crew energy) of "skunk" sets. Poor sets didn't matter as much. This efficiency was even more pronounced with a modern drum seiner. A fisherman didn't need to know too much about it all, he merely had to keep setting his net. Fishing on a drum seiner in the north, with long daylight hours, we made as many as many twenty sets in a day. There is an exception to this rule, however: fishermen who fished the lower Johnstone Straits were constrained by the fierce tides and made fewer sets on average. It all depended on where you were and when, and the fish. Much of modern fishing is "monkey see, monkey do," so the need for detailed knowledge has diminished over the years. But despite that, knowing tides, currents and fish gives you a decided advantage. We fishermen have always thought so.

## CHAPTER SEVEN

# THE PURETIC POWER BLOCK
# ON THE *WALTER M*, 1956

In 1956 I fished on the seiner FV *Walter M.* The boat was owned by Frank Hole in Coal Harbour on northern Vancouver Island and had been used previously in towing whales from the entrance of Quatsino Inlet through Quatsino Narrows to the whaling station in Coal Harbour. Because of his relationship with BC Packers (they had a share in the whaling station) he could charter the *Walter M* to the fishing side of their business. It was powered by the classic 85 horsepower Atlas Imperial engine and had a seine table and winch. In all these respects the *Walter M* was a nice old boat but it was to take on a new life as a salmon seiner using the newfangled Puretic power block.

This new technology was ultimately to transform the BC fisheries—and the world's. Previously, we pulled our net by hand, assisted by a powered roller on the table where the net was stowed. It was back-breaking work and the net was set only five or six times a day. Further, sets were planned and great care was taken to ensure they were successful. From a crewman's point of view we hated "blind sets," where the net was set when no one saw any sign of fish. We could see salmon when they jumped and became skilled at estimating the size of schools from their behaviour. Based upon the number and kind of jumpers we saw we could estimate our catch beforehand. If we didn't see any, we could guess that the set might not be worth the hard work. The Puretic power block was to change this dynamic. Blind sets were to become the norm.

Mario Puretic invented the power block and the technique it employed. Simply put, the net was attached to a revolving block and this brought it aboard with less muscle power being used. Rather than being pulled over the stern on the live roller, the net now descended onto the net table from the power block suspended high in the air on the boom. The problem we faced was how to get power to the block, and how we could make it revolve with enough power to bring in the net. Fortunately for our crew, others in BC had experimented with it the previous year and most of the major problems were solved. The net was set in the usual manner and pursed up as before. A small line was secured in the power block and it was attached to the end of the tow line. The block then pulled the net through it and onto the deck. It was then piled by the crew on the table.

On the *Walter M* we had a strange method—in retrospect it was pretty haywire but everything about the power block was new to us. The pulling power for the block was set up in a curious way. A special four-strand hard lay rope (line) was spliced to form a continuous loop and it was put in the pulley of the power block (on the outside, the net was inside) and the line was then wound around the winch with three or four turns. The line was tightened by a pulley placed between the winch and the power block. The pulley took up the slack in the line to ensure it would not slip in the power block. By engaging the winch, the line turned the power block and the net was pulled up out of the water and through the block down onto the net table. The same number of men were needed as with the old technique—one on the cork line (me), two or three on the web and one piling the lead line—but the work was substantially easier, piling the net rather than pulling it aboard.

Being a new technique, the kinks and wrinkles of using the Puretic power block had to be ironed out. Sometimes the line would stretch and the slack would cause backlashes on the winch and bring everything to a halt. The line had to be repositioned, the pulley tightened up and the winch engaged again. Sometimes the line would break and have to be re-spliced. It had to be done expertly (that is to say, neatly) so that no stray strands extruded from the splice to be caught on the winch, which would also cause backlashes.

A further problem arose: the net did not come in evenly. Sometimes there was too much cork line left in the water or the reverse, too much lead line left over. When pulling by hand the net came in evenly as each man could make the necessary adjustments to their part of the net. The solution to this problem was to tilt the power block with the hope that the cork line would ride higher, and so compensate for the fact that the cork line was longer than the lead line by about eighty feet (twenty-four metres), if the net was made in the conventional manner. Sometimes it worked. We continually experimented with the tilt and other adjustments to make it all perform efficiently. Being fishermen we had confidence in our ability to solve any sort of problem with the gear. We made it work because we had to.

The work was so much easier that we could not only make more sets in a day, but we would not be fatigued at the end of

FOLLOWING PAGE: The *Walter M* back when it was still powered by a heavy-duty Atlas Imperial four-cylinder engine, and before it was outfitted with a Puretic power block. UNIVERSITY OF BRITISH COLUMBIA, FISHERMAN PUBLISHING SOCIETY COLLECTION 1532/1184/1

the day. We were determined to make the technique work. There were some minor disadvantages, though. The men piling the net had to have good rain gear as they were continually deluged with water. Later in the summer, jellyfish occasionally appeared in our net and they had to be avoided. "Don't look up" was the mantra—the sting hurt! Canned milk was the lotion to be applied, and you had to be sure to wash your hands thoroughly before urinating.

In that long ago season of 1956 we started fishing in early July and within a few weeks we had mastered the new technology. Rather than making six sets of the net in a day and being tired out, we could make eight to ten and not be fatigued. We now could make money by fishing smaller schools, too. Before it might not have been economical to fish a certain area, but the new efficiency could make a difference. Most of the fleet was in Whales Channel; in the Namu area where we were fishing there were only about ten seiners. Lots of room to experiment.

We were fishing humpbacks (pink salmon). There are easy to fish as they move slowly—they are not fast and wild like sockeye—but at the same time their value is lower. We were more or less forced to fish pinks in the north, though, because 1956 was an off year for Adams River sockeye; they came every four years, and the next cycle year was 1958. The Namu area was new territory for us Johnstone Straits fishermen, so we moved to where there were few boats. This meant we fished Addenbrooke Light at the entrance to Fitz Hugh Sound, moved to Fish Egg Inlet sometimes and then moved up to fish around the south boundary of Koeye (pronounced "kway") River. If the swells were low we sometimes went to Hakai Pass.

What we were trying to do was figure out the movement of the fish. We then adjusted our fishing strategy to maximize our catch. So we would try Addenbrooke and if no fish in any numbers were coming we would move up to Fish Egg and see if any

Before the power block came into use, various methods were used to bring in nets. The technique shown here, called "fleeting," was used in the herring fishery because the nets were huge and heavy. CITY OF VANCOUVER ARCHIVES CVA 686-4638

schools were milling about, and then move up to Koeye. At Koeye we waited for the surge that came across from Hakai Pass, which brought the fish into what was back then known as "Jap Bay." Our catches were small but we didn't mind; we were young, and the Namu cannery had 150 women working in it and some of them were sure to find us attractive when we arrived on the weekends.

One set at Koeye River stands out in my memory for two reasons: it was a relatively big set and exciting because of that, but the set also had a result over forty years later. Here's how it all happened. At first light we were in Jap Bay and Willie Windsor on the *Miss Geraldine* was set for fish going to the river. Suddenly he turned the boat around and tried to reverse his net. This was strange. He was towing very hard and trying the almost impossible. We then saw why. Coming out of the little cove was a solid mass of fish that had backed out of the river and were schooled up there. I jumped into the skiff and we quickly set the net. The set was somewhat tricky as our spot was very shallow and the skipper didn't want to snag the net. It was not a normal setting spot. I only briefly tied the net to the beach as the skipper made a round set, encircling all the fish. We started pursing and the net was just black with fish. They were crowded into a small place as we only used part of the net in the set. We were excited, as this certainly was not a normal set. After pursing a while the winch stopped turning. We knew the problem: the power take-off on the front of the engine would slip and from time to time had to be tightened up. This meant the engine had to be stopped and it took about ten minutes for the skipper and me to fix the problem. All the while the crew madly plunged with their pole and pipe plungers into the net to keep the fish in it. We finished pursing, brought the net aboard and started brailing. We had about 7,200 salmon, although I always said it was a set of 8,000. It was the biggest set I had seen up to that time.

That set stuck in my memory for all the reasons above: first time using the Puretic power block, first time fishing the Namu area and the biggest set I had seen up to that time. But that set also had a sequel. In 2001 my friend and former skipper Byron Wright of the *Prosperity* told me he was going to fish a late opening in Area 8, the Namu area, precisely where we were in 1956. Ah, I said, let me tell you something from long ago. We got out the relevant chart and I showed him the set we had made forty years before. The fish school up in the river and then will come out on either side of the boundary. So a good strategy is to examine the little coves on either side of the river. Interesting, was his only comment. Well, I am sure by now you have guessed the result. Early in the morning (just like us) he was in Warrior Cove and set on the fish coming out of the cove. Not a bad set, he told me later. Not quite 18,000 pink salmon. Maybe in another forty years someone else will make that little set at Koeye River, at Jap Bay or Warrior Cove, take your choice.

The introduction of the Puretic power block was the first of many technological changes that transformed the industry. More efficiency meant more fish, more fish meant more money and more money led to investment in better boats. The fleet was to become bigger and better at catching fish. Further changes were to come but 1956 is the year I remember as the start of technological and economic changes I had not foreseen, and could not have. However, I did learn to drink a concoction called "porch climber." The drink consisted of a gallon of red wine into which you mixed a bottle of gin. It was said to be highly effective with the women in the Namu cannery. Maybe they were just bored. But I was twenty-one, a rough, tough fisherman pioneering a new fishing technology. Who could resist me? Or so I thought. The women and girls of the Namu cannery have all faded from my memory but that little set at Koeye River remains.

The large cannery in Namu had an ice plant and a reduction plant in addition to its canning lines. Once an important cannery, it later burned down and was abandoned. CITY OF RICHMOND ARCHIVES PHOTOGRAPH #1985 4 237

That 1956 season sticks in my memory for other reasons as well—one has to compare the good with the bad. Thinking of the previous fall I was reminded that fishing for a living is dangerous. As the good Doctor Johnson noted: being on a boat is like being in prison with the option of being drowned. Boats sink, men are washed overboard, lines snap and sometimes just standing up is a chore. The statistics are depressing but clear: fishing is one of the most dangerous occupations. While nature plays a part, conjuring up storms and rocks and reefs when they are not needed, human error also plays a role. Overloading boats increases the hazards, poor navigation puts boats on the rocks and tired men fall asleep at the wheel. Beach men like myself could fall out of the skiff, fall down on rocks or get hit by beach lines, among other perils. And sometimes we caused our own misfortune. I was a victim of a number of mistakes that would not have happened if we were using a Puretic power block rather than the old table seining method of pulling by hand. Technology does have its advantages.

In late 1955 I was a crewman on the FV *Cedric A*, skippered by Ronnie Myers. We were fishing in the lower Straits around Deepwater Bay in late October. We were after chum salmon ("dogs") but fish were few and the fall equinox had brought the southeast winds. A fierce storm was blowing. Ronnie's cousin Lawrence Myers was nearby with the FV *Ellen C*. Lawrence decided to set his net but soon got into trouble. Somehow he "lost his end," meaning he couldn't get the other end of the net to begin pursing. So he had the tow end of the net and tried to bring the other end of the net back, but couldn't. The crew was unable to do so — they just could not pull the net in by hand over the power roller as the wind was blowing the *Ellen* C away from the net. Their muscle power could not overcome the effect of the wind. They were in deep trouble in Deepwater Bay. Lawrence called Ronnie and said he desperately needed help. Unknown to us at the time one of the crew was in jail in Nanaimo so they were short-handed anyway. I volunteered to help.

The storm was horrendous; we could hardly stand up on the boat. It was impossible to go alongside the *Ellen* C as the two wooden boats would certainly be smashed. The plan was to put me into their skiff and I would get on the *Ellen* C. Their skiff was tied to their bow and with its long painter it was blown away

FOLLOWING PAGE: Back when I fished on the *Cedric A* in 1955, it had a power block. I almost drowned that season, when we tried to help another crew in Deepwater Bay, but lived to tell the tale. UNIVERSITY OF BRITISH COLUMBIA, FISHERMAN PUBLISHING SOCIETY COLLECTION 1532/555/1

from the *Ellen C.* This allowed Ronnie to come up to it with the *Cedric A.* He would put our bow up to the *Ellen C*'s skiff and I was to jump into it. That was the plan. Didn't work out that way.

The *Cedric A* was bouncing up and down in the swells and the *Ellen C*'s skiff was doing the same. I had to have perfect timing to jump from the bow into the skiff. My timing was wrong. When I jumped, a wave hit the skiff and moved it away from me and I was immediately in the ocean in Deepwater Bay. In the middle of a storm. Not good.

I was fully clothed with several layers on, heavy hip gumboots and luckily a surplus US Navy parka that I had done up at the neck. The parka in effect became a life preserver and the air in the parka held me up; it would have been impossible to swim with all that gear on me. Everyone looked on in helpless horror as I bobbled around in the water. But God does look after fools. The storm had swept the skiff away from me but in a few moments it came back at me and I desperately grabbed it and hauled myself in. I felt like a cold drowned rat and a foolish one at that. But I was in a safe, familiar place, a skiff. Soon I was aboard the *Ellen C* to much relief all around. I went into the fo'c'sle and put on the spare clothes I found there, which actually belonged to the crewman who was in jail, and went back onto the deck. After several hours we had the net back on the *Ellen C* and we headed into Granite Bay, where I reboarded the *Cedric A.* I took my wet clothes with me. I was still wearing someone else's clothes, but I felt it was a fair deal.

Whenever I ran into the jailed crewman he would always ask, "Where are my clothes?" I would always reply, "You got your crew share while in jail, didn't you?" It was a good trade. So we had an incident with a prison and a possible drowning. Doctor Johnson would have smiled. I never told my mother about any of it.

## CHAPTER EIGHT

# FISHING NIMPKISH
# DOG SALMON

At one time fishing was a simple occupation, never more so than in the Nimpkish dog salmon fishery. I fished them in 1959 aboard the FV *Moresby III*, owned and operated by Alfred "Boots" Jolliffe. Later I was to fish with his brother, Freddy, on the FV *Barkley Sound*. By November the main salmon fisheries were over and most boats had quit and put their nets into storage. But occasionally there would be a good return of Nimpkish dogs— so-called because they were bound for the nearby Nimpkish River, just across from Alert Bay. Such was the case in 1959 when Boots met me on the road in Alert Bay and said, "Want to come for a day or two and see what we can get?" Of course I wanted to.

Boots was an accomplished skipper and well respected because he was quiet, unassuming and had a reputation for getting fish when no one else could. Also, he was one of the few from the village who fished halibut with his boat in the early spring. The *Moresby III* was built in 1926 and lightly powered by an 88 horsepower Caterpillar engine, which was adequate for the light nets we used in those days. For dog salmon the net would often have three and half strips, but it would sometimes be deepened to four and a half strips, which was supposed to be more effective with dog salmon. We would use the Puretic power block system, too—no more exhausting hand-pulling. On this occasion, we had a two-day opening, Monday and Tuesday in early November.

So early Monday morning, in darkness, I got up and left my house on Pepper Point. A few doors down lived the cook, Johnny Lawson, and I knocked on his door. "Just a minute," he said and got out a small roast he had put in his fridge. This was to be lunch. Further along we called on Boots and we walked to the boat, which was tied at the dock near the Nimpkish Hotel. Jake Smith was already there and so was Ed "Gopher" Gordon. We had a full crew and left the dock in Alert Bay bound for the Johnstone Straits. It was cold and the prevailing southeast wind was blowing at about twenty-four knots. A light drizzle and overcast clouds made it a typical November day. Dog salmon weather, for sure. At dawn we were in Bauza Cove.

We always called Bauza Cove (see chart pages 90–91) "Bowser," not knowing how it got its name. Actually, it was named after one of the Spanish explorers who came this way at the time Captain Vancouver was also mapping the coast. We were not interested in maritime history, though, just where the fish were. Boots quietly informed me that the southeast winds sometimes blow the fish into Bauza Cove. Normally, few fish come into that little cove; most are below Blinkhorn, as the salmon are pushed out of Blackney Pass across the Straits on the big surges from big tides. On a very big tide they may be pushed back into Bauza Cove, as the big surges cause the current to reverse north. Boots figured that as the Nimpkish dogs are normally heading north, and a southeast was blowing, Bauza was a good bet. He was right. We saw them finning (not jumping, just showing their fins above water) very close to the gravel beach, but they were not moving. How to get them? We set the net in a semicircle around them,

Fishing on the *Moresby III*, with Boots Jolliffe at the helm and I believe my neighbour Johnny Lawson on the stern. Boots could catch fish when no one else could. We terrorized the Nimpkish dogs (chum salmon) in 1959. UNIVERSITY OF BRITISH COLUMBIA, FISHERMAN PUBLISHING SOCIETY COLLECTION 1532/1379/33

hoping they would move into our net. The skipper of the *Walter M*, another seiner, was watching us, and the fish, so he decided to help out. He went in close to the gravel beach next to the fish and made lots of noise by reversing his propeller. It worked. They came into our net.

Now we took the net aboard, and I felt good about bringing it in—no more pulling by hand. The net went up into the Puretic power block and came down onto the table. We merely had to stack it. I was on the cork line, Jake and Gopher piled the web and Johnny piled the lead line. Easy-peasy. Boots manned the controls to stop the power block if necessary, but there were no problems as we were an experienced crew.

We had fish. We lowered the brailer and dipped it into the net. We got a little over two hundred Nimpkish dog salmon. Nice work. We then had coffee and breakfast as Boots headed for Blinkhorn, where we would make another set. But we waited for signs of fish. We saw nothing, but the tide was good so we made a blind set. In the old days (three or four years before) we would have hated to do that because of the work but with the power block we didn't mind setting blind, as the work was minimal. This change foreshadowed the increase in efficiency that spelled some fundamental changes in the fishery. But at the time we didn't care about the future. The work was easier so we liked it.

The Blinkhorn set is easy. I have set there it seems a million times. I tied the net up to a familiar stump and watched intently for any sign of fish. It was cold, rainy and overcast, and I saw nothing. Boots closed up the net. Served us right for setting blind, only fifty fish. But we didn't mind.

It was an unusual fishery. We had only seen the *Walter M* and there were no other boats. Normally there would be about twenty or thirty in the Johnstone Straits but we were almost alone. If there were any fish we would get them. It was now high water so we moved across the Straits to try Buckaroo Bay, which was sometimes called the "Pig Ranch" for whatever reason. Fishermen give names to setting spots and sometimes you don't know how a place got its name. Just a few springs and two coho. No dogs. They weren't there. So we headed for Double Bay for the ebb tide.

I didn't like fishing in Double Bay even though we got a big set of humps there on the *Jean W* in 1953 that more or less paid for my first year at university. The reason was that the beach man had to tie to a rock that was a bit underwater. You also had to use two long beach lines as the net was set far offshore because of the bad bottom. But it was the best place to set in Double Bay. So we set. As in 1953 I was standing in a foot of water on the rock and trying to see fish. Again, we had set blind. I saw one jumper so maybe there would be fish. Finally, Boots signalled me to let the beach line go and Jake came and got me in the skiff and we rowed out to the *Moresby*. We brought the net aboard, dried up the bunt and we had a nice set, over three hundred dog salmon. That was more like it. So we did it all again. I was missing lunch but I didn't mind, we were getting fish and there could be more. And there were: we had over two hundred fish in the net. But the third set was a bust. So we moved.

We took a look in Mitchell Bay and saw no jumpers, and Boots remarked that it didn't look "fishy" so we moved to Rough Bay, and made a set off the Sointula government dock. I told Boots not to drop the beach end too close to the wharf as we had netted a bedspring and a bicycle once when fishing there for sockeye. I was on the *Jean W* at the time. In the end it was nice little set, over a hundred dogs. But it was dark by then and we headed for home. We kept the fish overnight.

The next morning was colder and more blustery. The wind was picking up. Boots didn't want to go to the Straits because it was really looking like a big blow was coming. So we headed for Rough Bay again. We also looked at Haddington Reef, as sometimes the salmon like to hang around there. In those days we believed, and rightly so, that dog salmon liked to hang around reefs and drive fishermen nuts—you couldn't set on them without the possibility of snagging your net. A "skunk" (no fish) was the usual result of that strategy. Nothing was showing on the reef so we headed to Sointula and set again off the government dock, catching sixty or seventy fish. So we tried again, tying to the dock and watching for jumpers, hoping for the same. No luck. By noon Boots had had enough. "There's nothing here, boys," he said. So we went to the BC Packers dock in Alert Bay and stripped our net. That was the end of the season for us.

Boots's seine was the type used before nylon became common, that is, it was made of cotton web and manila lines. It had to be handled with care to avoid rotting, and required the net to be stripped each year. The lines were cut off and the lacing holding the strips together was cut out to separate the hundred-mesh strips. We put the cork and lead lines on a pallet and put the strips of web into a large bluestone tank. Bluestone was copper sulphate crystals, which were put into a tank with sea water. This killed all the algae ("feed") on the web. We left the web strips in the tanks overnight and the next day we hung them up in Boots's net locker, where next year they would be hauled down and a new net built in the manner we always did.

About a week later Boots said: "Your settlement cheque is ready at the office." I went upstairs at the BC Packers office and got a cheque for $212 for the two days. Nowadays that money would be worth over ten times that, that is, about $2,400 dollars. So in today's terms I made over $1,000 a day. Thanks, Boots.

## CHAPTER NINE

# PIT-LAMPING ON THE *VANISLE*, 1963

In the 1960s I helped to almost wipe out the Pacific herring in BC. The fishery was so successful the government had to close it for a few years until the stocks recovered. My role was a minor one; I was a crewman on the BC Packers seiner the FV *Vanisle*. We were in the 1963 summer herring fishery and the crew and captain were from Alert Bay. The skipper was my neighbour, Freddy Jolliffe. We hoped to make some extra money before the salmon season. It was going to be interesting as it was a new fishery for me.

A very efficient technique had evolved to attract the last of the herring. Rather than hunting for them the usual way, this new method brought the fish right to the net. "Pit-lamping" entailed the use of lights and a specialized method of catching them at night. The term came from the technique of using miner's lamps (pit lights) to kill deer at night. Many Alert Bay fishermen were familiar with that hunting technique and the use of lights in the herring fishery saw the term transferred.

The technique required very strong lights that were usually fitted to the upper superstructure on either side of the boat. The lights were standard sodium street lights or other similar types.

In addition, a small gas generator was placed in an extra "dead skiff" (it had no motor) and two lamps were put in it. The fish boat towed the two skiffs behind it while fishing: one with an engine, the power skiff, and one without, the dead skiff. The larger "home" vessel, in this case the *Vanisle*, had the usual large herring seine and a Puretic power block for bringing in the net. With boats outfitted in such a way, herring fishermen could use the new technique, much to the detriment of the herring stocks. In fact pit-lamping was too efficient and was soon banned, and the herring fishery closed. My role in this was minor, as I said, but I was there.

I came out of university in early May of 1963 just in time for the summer herring reduction fishery to start and went aboard the FV *Vanisle*, which was a classic double-decker with its small pilothouse on top and painted in the standard ugly BC Packers colours. It was capable of packing a hundred tons of herring and my share, at two dollars per ton, would be two hundred dollars for a full load. Big money. The *Vanisle* had only minimal navigation equipment: a compass and an Ekolite paper recording sounder—critical in the fishery, but nothing compared to modern-day sonar. This set-up was standard in the industry at that time. The wooden power skiff was the normal gas-powered type, painted red, as usual. Fred Jolliffe was the skipper and the crew was made up of experienced men, not Freddy's usual salmon crew from his boat the FV *Barkley Sound*. I knew everyone and everyone knew me.

In those days the herring fishery was open from two p.m. Sunday to Friday at two p.m. There was some logic behind the schedule but I forget what it was. Anyhow, we would put the grub aboard early Sunday morning and leave Alert Bay and head for the fishing grounds. Our favourite spots were Hope Island and Nigei Island at the top end of Vancouver Island. If we left

Alert Bay at about noon we were there by late afternoon and could start cruising. The procedure was simple: look for signs of fish. Birds, unusual currents, other boats or anything at all. The Ekolite sounder was going continuously. If it detected fish a black mark appeared on the sounder. Locating and catching the fish required some special expertise. We would later take our fish to the reduction plant in Namu, across Queen Charlotte Sound.

The *Vanisle* cruised continually with its sounder on. Cheap fuel made extensive cruising possible. In the pilothouse were two men: the skipper, Freddy, and me on the wheel. When a black

The *Vanisle* was a standard BC Packers double-decker. Using an Ekolite paper sounder and street lights, we pit-lamped herring for fishmeal and oil in 1963—and in doing so helped to almost wipe them out. UNIVERSITY OF BRITISH COLUMBIA, FISHERMAN PUBLISHING SOCIETY COLLECTION 1532/1166/1

mark appeared on the Ekolite sounder it signalled herring, but we didn't know how many and exactly where they were. Except we knew they were beneath the boat. Once we detected herring, the procedure was to turn hard to starboard (we always set the net clockwise) and make a circle and come back up on the school. To help locate the school I used to toss balls of coloured paper over the side as soon as I got a black mark on the sounder. When I came back up on the fish after circling I could see where I had been by looking for the coloured paper on the surface of the water.

Because we were working in strong currents the wake of the vessel was not a circle but more of an ellipse. Herring, while feeding, usually "bucked the tide" (swam against it) so when you found them and made your turns you were at first going with the tide and then coming back you were going against it. This ellipse made finding the original fish difficult. The turning circumference could be as much as half a mile (up to a kilometre). The fish might have moved, or you could miss your target. I fancied myself as being good at this technique as Freddy never replaced me on the wheel. After several turns and many bits of paper and markings on the sounder we usually had a good idea of the size of the school, where it was and how it was acting. When Freddy felt all was ready he pulled a wooden handle located above the wheel, which sounded a horn, and the skiffs were let go. We were setting the net, again in the traditional clockwise manner.

Setting a 300-fathom (550-metre) herring seine that was 26 strips (about 70 metres) deep was tricky business. One mistake and the net was lost, and with it perhaps the season. The company frowned upon skippers who snagged or lost their seines. It was rare, but always a present danger. Usually we made the standard circle set described above during daylight, as we knew where the school was. Freddy was especially good at "open sets" where the power skiff towed the net and then closed it up. This procedure

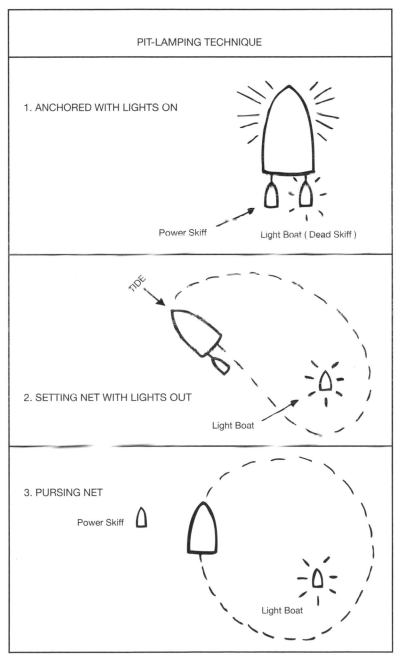

This is how we pit-lamped herring in the 1960s before it was banned as it also took immature salmon.

was used to catch travelling fish we could see on the surface. Once we saw that they were inside the net we closed up.

Bringing the net aboard with a Puretic power block followed a certain familiar routine. We used a wire purse line and pursed both ends, and spooled the wire onto small revolving drums located on deck. Once the net was pursed up we attached clamps ("come-alongs") to the two lines in the davit and then lifted the lead line onto the deck. This technique was later supplanted by the use of "ring-strippers," which held the purse rings on an iron bar attached to the bulwarks. The purse line was taken out of the rings and we could then bring in the net. At the same time the power skiff was attached by a small towing bridle to the *Vanisle*, and the skiff man towed us out of our net; otherwise the net would have surrounded the boat while we brought it in. The dead skiff was tied alongside.

Once we had most of the net aboard we usually put the dead skiff on the cork line and then dried up the net, getting it ready for brailing. By using straps and lifting lines we tightened the bag of fish. It was necessary to work carefully as the net could burst. The mantra was "keep the knots even." This meant to dry up the net so that the strain was evenly—repeat evenly—distributed in the net's bunt, which was the heavier web at the end of the net. When we had dried up to Freddy's satisfaction we started to get the herring aboard. We used a brailer capable of holding two tons of herring on each dip. We prided ourselves on being good at it. We would dip the brailer, the *Vanisle* would heel over from the two tons of weight and we would then lift the brailer out of the net, send it across the deck and release the catch. The herring would spill into the hold and as the *Vanisle* righted itself it would roll back to the starboard side and we would dip the brailer again. When done right this process was all one fluid motion. After fifty or more dips we had a load, and the hatches were battened down. We had wooden hatch boards, and over them we put a canvas and then two "strongbacks," timbers clamped down to hold the hatch boards in place as we travelled. We were then bound for Namu, where the herring reduction plant was located. We had to make an 80-mile (128-kilometre) journey across Queen Charlotte Sound to get to the plant.

If fishing during the day was slow it was time to use the lights. Darkness was our friend, and ideally there would be no moon. Great care was taken in choosing where to use the lights as working in the dark increased the potential for bad things to happen. Once a suitable spot was found we anchored and the engine was shut down. The presence of small scattered schools of "skim" herring on the surface early in the night was a good indicator of fish in the area. The Ekolite sounder showed us that. Anchor down, we usually had supper and then set up for the night. The attracting lights were lit on the *Vanisle*, and the gas electric generator started in the dead skiff and its lights also turned on. Now we waited. After several hours it was time to check if fish had come to the lights. If it looked good the power skiff was sent out to sound the school, as it had a small sounder aboard also. If Freddy figured all was good we would set the net. But this required a certain careful procedure.

First, noise was our enemy. It spooked the herring. No slamming of doors, no dropping of wrenches, no banging on the hull, those were the orders. The engineer wanted to start the main engine with a minimum of noise so he engaged the starter only briefly (its noise was "bad") and he got the main engine going as quickly as possible. This noise caused the fish to surge away from the boat and then we waited for them to come back to the lights. Once we were sure they were back we went on to the next step. It was now time to lift the anchor. This was also done with a minimum of noise. The cable was spooled on the anchor winch but the anchor chain was

This photograph of the *Vanisle* shows the layout of the deck and the net as it was in 1962, using a power block. Note the two skiffs. In this shot, herring are being pumped out. DON PEPPER

left hanging overboard with the anchor. A red mark on the cable told us when to stop spooling. Spooling the anchor chain in its chock was just too noisy, and scared the fish away.

With the anchor up but hanging overboard, it was time to make our move. The lights of the *Vanisle* were turned off and only those in the dead skiff were left on. After a short time and anxiety all around the vessel's clutch was engaged and the *Vanisle* slowly crept away from the fish, leaving behind the dead skiff with its lights on. This procedure shifted the fish from the *Vanisle's* lights to the dead skiff's lights. The dead skiff "held" the fish.

Once the *Vanisle* was a suitable distance from the fish, Freddy blew the horn and the net was let go, being pulled off the stern by the power skiff. The dead skiff meanwhile was left encircled by the net; once the net was closed up and we were pursing, the power skiff went and got the dead skiff, rowing it over the cork line and back to the *Vanisle*. If it all worked out, and it usually did, we would have a load of herring. The skipper's great skill and a competent crew made it all work. I was fortunate to be in the pilothouse with the skipper, where I could observe the whole operation.

We spent most of the time cruising, looking for fish. It was very pleasant. One time when I was on the wheel, Freddy said "Follow that bird," and pointed to an eagle flying to somewhere offshore. I did and we found a school of herring in the Deserters Group, remote islands far offshore. Freddy reasoned that an eagle flying over the sea must have a reason and that reason was herring.

I was once the victim of a sly move by the skipper of the FV *Waldero*, a well-known successful and aggressive fisherman. I was on the wheel and circling a school of herring while Freddy was dealing with an issue on deck. I kept circling and watching the sounder to be sure I was on the fish. Suddenly I heard the loud horn of a herring seiner setting. The *Waldero* was setting in my wake. He only had to follow my circle and he got the fish. Ouch! Freddy just said "That's a smart fisherman," but I wondered what he really thought of me.

It was not all work and no play, especially with one of the crewmen, Freddy's nephew. The devil finds work for idle hands. After a successful night set that loaded us, the Newfie cook promised up a wonderful breakfast. Sure enough, eggs, bacon, sausages, fried potatoes, toast, coffee and as an added treat, pancakes. Unfortunately the cook had not mastered the art of making hotcakes on his stove. They were horrible. After this breakfast we battened down the hatches, attached the canvas covering and put on the strongbacks to hold the hatch boards in place. We then headed to the reduction plant in Namu. While at the dock I was talking to the men unloading the fish. They said, what is up with that guy? The Newfie cook was running along the side of the *Vanisle* ripping at something. He then saw me and above the noise of the unloading equipment I could hear him yelling and swearing at me. The reason? Someone had taken about eight pancakes, punched a hole in their centres, attached a piece of hanging twine and hung them along the *Vanisle* as bumpers! The cook was highly incensed and never forgave me for the prank. But it was not me, it was Freddy's nephew. Still funny after all these years.

In all, fishing for herring was a great experience, and I learned a lot during that season on the *Vanisle*. Being in the wheelhouse and seeing how the decisions were made about when and where to set our net was special. But we were too good at it. We were wiping out the fish. The technique had to be banned and the herring fishery shut down for about ten years. We were killing not only all the mature herring but also immature herring and salmon. After the summer we took the *Vanisle* back to Celtic Shipyards and got our salmon seine and put it on the *Barkley Sound*, Freddy's own boat. Herring was done with; it was time for salmon, but that is another thing. I had to wait almost thirty years to fish herring again.

Thinking back to Freddy's nephew and the pranks he would come up with reminds me of another incident that I like to call the story of the "extra crewman on the *W R Lord*." Fishing was hard work with many risks. There was no guarantee of fish and the dangers of the sea were always there. To offset this situation, cheerfulness and high spirits would sometimes break out. In 1961 I was on the FV *W R Lord* with Captain Vern Skogan as the beach man. We left Kelsey Bay at about noon on a Sunday and headed north to start fishing in the Johnstone Straits. Fishing would open at six p.m. so we were cruising and looking for fish. We went into Glorious Bay (St. Vincent Bay on the charts, an hour or so north) when Vern saw a small black bear on the beach. Being an excellent shot he killed it with one bullet. Go get the bear he said to me, as I was the beach man. I got into the skiff, went to the beach and prodded the bear with an oar to be sure he was dead. He was, and I loaded him into the skiff and he was soon hoisted aboard the *Lord* for the photo session. I was for some reason disgusted with all this. Killing a bear just to take photos didn't seem right.

When the photo session was done Vern told me to throw the bear overboard. I didn't, wanting to be somehow perverse. What do you do with a dead bear? Well, you dress him up in spare oilskins, yellow pants and a green jacket and top it all off with a black sou'wester. Then I tied him in the rigging, at the bulwarks by the mast stays just back of the cabin. He looked like a small crewman surveying the horizon. There I left him.

Fishing was good on Sunday night and we fished until dark. The crew of various boats that came close obviously wondered who the extra crewman was and upon a closer look, laughed. The same prevailed all the next day and the day after that. By now half

147

the fleet knew there was an extra "man" on the *W R Lord*. But by Wednesday Vern told me to get rid of the bear as he was beginning to stink. I promised to do so. Late that night we went into Growler Cove to anchor up but decided instead to tie alongside the *Barkley Sound*, whose crew had their anchor down, their lights out and were sleeping. Vern and the skipper of the *Barkley Sound* had married two sisters so it was no problem tying alongside, they were family. We did all the nice things, tied up quietly and shut down our engine immediately. Everyone but me went to bed.

I had a higher purpose. I took the little bear down from the rigging, wrestled him across our deck onto the *Barkley Sound* and into their galley. In the darkness I placed him in the skipper's seat, putting a coffee cup in his right hand and a comic book in the other. I even placed a cigarette in his mouth. There I left him. I retired for the night. We left before the crew of the *Barkley* were awake so I was not able to get their response. I was severely disappointed with them, as we came close several times during the day but received no words of anger or amusement. I considered them spoilsports.

Fishing closed at six p.m. so we went home to Alert Bay to deliver our fish to the fish packers. We finished about ten o'clock so I had just enough time to go up to the Legion and have a few drinks, and see if there were any young nurses there from the hospital. I fancied myself a Lothario, as all young men do. It was quiet so I went back down to the *W R Lord* to go to sleep. It was about one a.m. so I was very quiet getting into the fo'c'sle, so as not to disturb the other crewmen. I slipped gently into my bunk. Well, it was not a woman in a fur coat in my bed. My friend from Glorious Bay was with me. I gave my little shipmate a burial at sea the next day.

## CHAPTER TEN

# Hard Times:
# A Tough Season Drum Seining
# on the *BC Maid*
# and a Bad Year Gillnetting

In 1969 I fished salmon on the FV *BC Maid*. She was a nice little old table seiner, built in 1926, that had been converted into a drum seiner. Drum seining was a new technique, said to be invented by a man in Sointula who adapted the idea of the gillnetter's net drum to seining. In effect, the net was wound onto a large drum rather than being pulled by hand onto a net table or stacked on the net table using a Puretic power block. Using the new technique required a number of adjustments, however, using the old fishing process of trial and error.

Many modifications had to be made not only to the vessel but also to the net. In adapting the *BC Maid* to drum seining the table was removed and a well was made in the stern, under the drum. It was made of welded steel. The purpose was to lower the drum's centre of gravity; otherwise the net would be several feet higher in the air, obviously affecting the stability of the vessel. The drum sat partially in the well. Next, power had to be applied to the drum. In this case a hydraulic pump running from the power take-off on the front of the main engine supplied power to a truck transmission mounted on the deck just behind the drum. A chain ran from the transmission to a large gear on the drum. The transmission had several gears so we could make sure the right amount of power would go to the drum. This was a hybrid set-up and was prone to malfunction. Somewhat haywire was one comment.

To complete the set-up a horizontal piece was added on the stern. It was a steel roller, about eight inches (twenty centimetres) in diameter, over which the net would travel when it was being spooled on the drum. Behind the roller was a metal track over which the spooling gear ran. The track consisted of two upright rollers that guided the net as it was spooled across the drum. This mechanical set-up allowed for a significant change in how the net was pursed. Previously, on a table seiner, both ends of the net were pursed so that the middle of the net was where it was finally tightened. The drum seining technique allowed a change in pursing. Only one end was pursed, the bunt or final end. The single purse line was now attached to the lead line about two-thirds of the way along the net. Upon closing the net the drum started rolling and brought in the net while the other end was pursed. Once the net was fully pursed ("the rings are up"), the rings were placed on a steel hook ("the hairpin") and drumming continued. The purse line was piled on deck and ran through the rings as the net was being spooled. This technique allowed for faster sets of the net because our pursing time was significantly shortened and the drum brought in the net faster than the Puretic power block. A significant side benefit for the crew was that little or no muscle power was required. When it worked as designed it was slick.

The drum seining technique also required a change in the

Here is the *BC Maid* looking pretty good, after Oley Skogan fixed it up. Fishing on the *BC Maid* in 1969 was my worst season, but most interesting. Three of us tried to do the work of five men, and with lousy equipment to boot. CITY OF RICHMOND ARCHIVES #1999·6·159

hanging of the net. Before, a net was more or less hung at 20 percent. This meant that 240 fathoms of web were hung onto about 200 fathoms of cork line. The lead line was also shorter than the cork line by about 12 fathoms. This design ensured a "bag" of web ballooning out from the cork line and was supposed to increase catching ability. This net design caused problems on a drum seiner, though. The extra web was a problem, causing backlashes and ripping the web as the net came off the drum. But worse was the tendency for the lead line to tightly roll up the web onto it. It was a mess and difficult to unwind by hand. These roll-ups could be several fathoms long and they raised that part of the net up so that fish could easily go under the net. Also, they looked horrible. The solution to these problems was to hang the net "flatter" with less percentage of web, about 10 percent. Also, the lead line was lengthened a little. The exact way in which the drum seine nets were hung was a dark secret, with everyone experimenting with different combinations to get it right. One small change in setting seemed to help in overcoming lead line and cork line roll-ups. The procedure was to set the net in a slow, small arc, avoiding sharp turns in the net. It took several years to perfect the technique but the obvious advantages of drum seining saw it quickly adopted by the salmon fleet. Our set-up on the *BC Maid* was somewhat unique but the overall method was the same for all.

We were three: skipper Byron Wright, at twenty-three, Oley Skogan, the same age, and me, slightly older. We had made a pact that whoever became skipper first, the others would support him by being crew. The big problem for neophyte skippers was getting experienced men. Also, a normal crew was five. Our plan was to

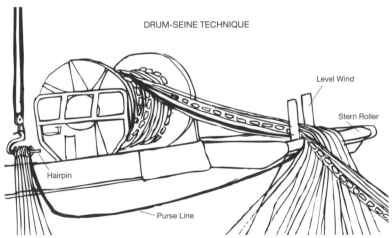

This sketch shows how a drum seiner brings the net back onto the drum. The hairpin holds the purse rings and the lead line out of the water.

fish with only three and thereby make more money by splitting the other two shares. We had discussed this plan many times as crewmen on other boats. It meant that we would have to each work harder and somehow make three become five. We split the tasks. Byron was skipper so that was the total of his job description. Oley was in charge of all things mechanical and he worked his magic daily on the ancient engine and our haywire set-up. My job was threefold: skiff man, beach man and cook. Setting the net required me rowing the skiff and leaping ashore to tie up the net. Oley operated the drum. We made it work. But it was exhausting Ultimately, we would hire young boys to help out and pay them a small wage, or nothing at all. John Macko from Alert Bay was our first extra man; I think he was about fourteen. He was assigned to me in the skiff. He was fast learner and I tried to get him to cook as well but he just gave me a blank stare, meaning no way.

Byron soon became adept at setting the net so we had minimal roll-ups and didn't get into too many "jackpots"—collapsed sets with the net all around the boat or ripped on the rocks in a bad set. Byron was always experimenting, setting in places where no one had before. The ability to get the net back faster than usual allowed him to take chances in new places. At such times Oley merely rolled his eyes and said nothing.

Byron was impatient to become successful and catch lots of fish. To that end we set and set and set our net. In the traditional spots this was a no-brainer but Byron wanted to try new places, and try them using the new drum seining technique. This led us out to the Deserters Group, a cluster of islands in the middle of Queen Charlotte Sound, unproven grounds. There to our surprise was Boots Jolliffe on the *Moresby III*. He still used the Puretic power block technique. We went alongside and asked Boots how to fish there. Normally this was just not done, but Byron was new and Boots was kindly. So he told us where to set and cautioned us:

153

after he set his net, we had to let him get pursed up and out of the way as the tidal surge came and pushed everything towards some rocks. So Boots set his net and was pursing but Byron couldn't wait. So we set, too soon as it turned out. The surge hit us as we were pursing and pushed the two boats and the nets together. It was a colossal mess. Both crews used poles and muscle power to separate the two nets—somehow some of our net had ended up in Boots's net and he had pursed it up inside his.

Oley and I were disgusted with all this, as Boots had warned us. His crew also gave us poisonous looks, having heard the conversation. Eventually we got untangled and Byron said thank you to Boots. Boots in his usual pleasant manner remarked that the surge "sure made things goofy." No "I told you so" or any reprimand to Byron. Such was his nature. You can also note Byron's.

That season on the *BC Maid*, we were reminded that the perils of fishing are many. One special case that springs to mind is the time when we made a set at "Soldier Point." (On the charts this is called Lady Ellen Point but we never called it that. Fishermen often have their own names for places.) I was familiar with this setting place, as I had fished it in the early 1950s when fishing Nimpkish sockeye. It was a tricky spot to set, requiring the beach man and the skiff man to let the beach end of the net go several times, tie it up again and repeat the process. The reason was that the tide shoved the end of the net up onto the gravel beach. When about five fathoms of net were on the beach, the beach man let the end go and raced along the beach in his clumsy gumboots to tie the net to the next convenient tree. He then repeated the process. It was crucial to get the third and last tie up or the strong tide would push the end of the net onto a rock pile, causing the net to snag and rip. Not good.

So one fine August day in 1969 we set the net at Soldier

Point. What could go wrong? By now we were experienced with drum seining on the *BC Maid* and we had added John Macko to our crew, who was young, but willing. He was on the beach with me. I tied up to the first tree and waited for the tide to push the net onto the gravel beach. My tie-up technique was old-fashioned, consisting of looping wraps of beach line around the tree. (The "magic knot" used on poly lines was still to come.) Several minutes later it was time to let it go, as the tide was strong and pushing the net onto the beach. I underestimated the strength of the tide. When I let the last wrap go it swung around the tree and a bight of line hit me in the stomach, knocking me down.

Seeing the problem John grabbed the beach line and wrapped it around the next tree, which I had pointed out to him. I lay on the beach, slowly recovering. Soon the tide did its business and John, when he let the beach line go, suffered the same fate as me. Looking on, Byron saw his two men laying on the beach, apparently knocked out, and his net quickly drifting to the rock pile. He was helpless. I recovered, however, and ran down the beach, and was able to make the last tie-up tree. We went back aboard the *BC Maid* with sore bodies. John's only comment to Byron was: "Let's not set there again, eh?" And we never did.

The *BC Maid* was to be the last wooden seiner I fished on. The 1969 season was one of the worst I ever had. I left fishing to get married and take a job on land. By that time I had a graduate degree and a job teaching economics at BC Institute of Technology. Somehow or other Oley and Byron must have continued to work their magic, because in 1970 the *BC Maid* was one of the top boats for BC Packers. I was a year too early.

The next year, 1970, improbably, I returned to fishing in the summer, while I was off from my teaching position at BCIT. Like most things, it seemed a good idea at the time. My wife and I lived on the Ladner dyke and I had bought a small beat-up gillnetter called the *Tike*. The plan was to fish the Fraser River, right on my doorstep. But the fishing was terrible in the river so I made the decision to head to my old stomping grounds, the Johnstone Straits. Back in 1947 I made my first set at Izumi Rock in the Straits. I was thirteen years old and I was with Henry ("Hank") Myers on his little Easthope-powered double-ended gillnetter, the *Hawk*. He was older than me, sixteen, and how he got the *Hawk* I never knew. We loaded up with food: bacon and eggs, canned beans, bread and jam. As it happened, we got about thirty fish, sockeye, and the result was that I knew how to fish the Izumi Rock set on a gillnetter.

In 1970, some twenty-three years later, I did it again. I had my thirty-three-foot (ten-metre) gillnetter, the *Tike*, powered by a Chrysler Crown gas engine and the wrong sort of net. I had a light Fraser River net but I figured I could use it in the Straits. I foresaw no problems, having seined there for many years. It was, in effect, my own backyard, as I could see my former home on Cormorant Island from Blinkhorn. So in early August I was there and at dark on the night in question I threw over the float with the lantern on the end of the net and paid out the net in a straight line out into the Straits, and I remembered to put a little hook in the end to catch any salmon that didn't want to gill and tried to go around the net. I was now "hanging on the end" of my net and made myself a cup of tea on the Coleman stove. Not much had changed in twenty-three years.

In the pitch dark I slowly drifted towards Blinkhorn and watched for dangers, and I soon had one. I could see the lights of a tugboat with a tow heading south, obviously a log barge coming at me at about fifteen knots. I was not close to shore but in the middle of the Straits, the "steamboat channel" as we called it. It was my obligation to leave a clear path for the tugboat, but

I didn't want to pick up my net so I took a chance. If he ran over my net it would be very bad for me: the net would be destroyed, and it could cause him problems if my net got in his propeller. I anxiously watched as he sailed by the end of my net. I could still see my lantern between him and me so I was clear. Not much fun in the dark. After several hours I unhooked the net and ran along it from one end to the other, partly to scare fish into the net and also to see how it was fishing. I saw lots of fish and got excited. I knew the tide was changing and that the surge from the flood tide would soon come out of Blackney Pass and bring with it lots of salmon. So I waited. I could actually hear the surge of the tide.

I watched the lantern at the end of my net do some crazy gyrations and knew that meant the surge was hitting it. I anticipated lots of fish and started to pick up my net. Immediately I had a problem a thirty-foot (nine-metre) log hopelessly entangled in my net. I decided to let the tide carry me across the Straits into Bauza Cove and deal with the problem in daylight in the morning. I would pick out my fish and clear up the mess in my net. Once in the cove I dropped the hook and waited for daylight to see the extent of my problem. I went to sleep, for perhaps three or four hours, then heard a horn from a seine boat waking me up. It was some of my old friends on the *Barbara K*, a seiner out of Alert Bay. They had a hearty laugh at my predicament and said I should have stuck to seining. They were right. My net was a complete mess. It had not only the log, but also a good assortment of driftwood, kelp and garbage. It took me all day to clear the mess. Now I faced a weekend of net mending.

My career of fishing Izumi Rock with a gillnet was over. I left for Ladner and Fraser River fishing. I had my teaching job to return to in September so I ended my gillnetting career completely, and none too soon. I sold the gillnetter to some Americans in Bellingham.

Those two years of hard times brought home to me the perils of fishing. Risk and uncertainty are your constant companions. My prosperous years had given me the money to go to university in

This classic canoe stern gillnetter is similar to the one I owned in 1970. Later, a flatter transom stern was standard. IMAGE I-27845 COURTESY OF ROYAL BC MUSEUM, BC ARCHIVES

the winter. I find it somewhat incredible now but in the 1960s I was able to fish in the summer, fly to England to go to university during term time and then fly back to BC to go fishing again. Without student loans—I could finance it all myself from fishing. I did so for three years, and like all gamblers I thought the good times would never end. The hard data says I made slightly over eight hundred dollars in 1969 and had a loss of several thousands in 1970. There was a lesson I was forced to grasp. Fishing is a risky business.

## CHAPTER ELEVEN

# FISHING THE BLUE LINE

Every fishing area on the coast has its own peculiarities, which guide how you would fish there. But the "Blue Line" fishery in Juan de Fuca Strait was highly specialized. It was called the Blue Line after the line on the ice in hockey. There were restrictions on how you could enter that zone, so it was only natural that a fishing boundary that had a "no go" area would end up being called the Blue Line. It turned out to be a unique fishery, one that to me epitomized the challenges of fishing. To be successful you had to be good, and often lucky. With good gear and experience, however, you could make your own luck, as is the case in other endeavours.

For over fifty years, to be a Blue Line fisherman meant you were part of the elite. Now it is no more, as the highly controlled quota fishery of today allows each vessel to get a defined share. But when I fished the Blue Line it was more or less a "dog eat dog" fishery. Every man for himself and the devil take the hindmost. The result was an exciting fishery at which we, meaning the captain and crew of the *Prosperity*, excelled. Our mantra was: "Success comes when preparation meets opportunity."

Some background is necessary. Usually fishing boundaries

were located around the mouths of the salmon rivers, those scattered up and down the coast. But a new boundary, and a new fishery, for salmon fishermen was introduced back in the 1950s. It came about because Canada and the US had a fisheries agreement for Fraser River sockeye, whereby both nations contributed to maintaining the run and shared the catch. The Pacific Salmon Commission, a joint effort, was charged with managing the fishery. The US had invested in building the Hell's Gate fish ladders on the Fraser and so earned their share of the catch. However, there was no treaty on pink salmon. The Canadian fisheries minister at that time, James Sinclair, tried to get the US to agree to sharing all the fish, not only the sockeye, but also the pinks that went through Juan de Fuca Strait (a body of water shared by both nations). For a variety of reasons he could not get any sort of an agreement.

In a bold stroke Sinclair allowed Canadian fishermen to buy large surplus sardine vessels from the collapsed US fishery. Then he encouraged the Canadian fleet to fish relatively far out to sea on the so-called "Bonilla–Tatoosh Line," which ran from the Bonilla Light in Canada to the US's Tatoosh Island. This was a boundary beyond which the fleet could not go. However, it was at the front of where the fish first entered the Juan de Fuca Strait. By fishing there you could, in theory, catch almost all the fish going to the Fraser River. Very few fish entered Juan de Fuca on the US side of the strait because of the peculiarities of fish behaviour.

The Bonilla–Tatoosh boundary (the aforementioned Blue Line) was closely patrolled by Canadian fisheries vessels and if you went over the line you had to dump your catch and you could possibly be fined for fishing in the "closed area." Sinclair's strategy was ultimately successful as the Canadian fleet in theory could, as I said, catch all the pink salmon bound for the Fraser River. The US soon came to the table to negotiate. They wanted to ensure their catch of the pinks for their Puget Sound fisheries. But the Blue Line fishery remained for us Canadians.

I first fished the Blue Line in 1963 aboard the *Barkley Sound*. Realistically we were too small a boat to fish out there, only sixty-five feet (twenty metres) in length fishing against over seventy-five-foot (twenty-three-metre) double-deckers. However, we could pack a west coast seine, which was larger and deeper than our "inside" seine—1,000 feet (300 metres) rather than 650 feet (200 metres) and over eight strips of web compared to five and three-quarters strips. We had to tow our power skiff, though, as the *Barkley* would have surely sunk with all that extra weight of both the net and the skiff on it. Being smaller and less seaworthy we fished "behind the line," or not far from Sooke Harbour, and mainly around Sheringham Light. The ocean swells were much smaller there and we preferred calm seas. The larger boats fished in front of us, "on the line." Surprisingly, we did well, as there was a run of very large pinks, over five pounds, rather than the usual three-and-a-half- or four-pounders. But it was no fun. We pitched and rolled and just standing up was a struggle, but we had to fish and so we did.

Fishing behind the line was easy, in a way. With lots of space you could set anywhere and at anytime within the twelve-hour (six a.m. to six p.m.) opening. The drawback was that the larger boats in front of you scooped up most of the fish, so in the late afternoon the catches dropped off. Nonetheless, we could make five or six sets a day and welcome Sooke Harbour at seven p.m. We fished there again another season with the *Barkley Sound* but it was a disaster in that we got few fish, the run was poor and the crewmen were unhappy. Somehow, I ended up as cook and engineer, a combination not usually seen, as fuel oil and olive oil don't mix. I swore never to go back to that fishery unless I was on a boat as big as the *Queen Mary*. The future had other ideas.

In the 1960s, "Fearless" Fred Jolliffe twice took us to Juan de Fuca Strait on the *Barkley Sound* to fish the Blue Line using a west coast seine and a power skiff. It was not for the fainthearted—we were perhaps the smallest boat fishing there. UNIVERSITY OF BRITISH COLUMBIA, FISHERMAN PUBLISHING SOCIETY COLLECTION 1532/467/1

In 1987 I returned to the Blue Line aboard the FV *Prosperity*, which was owned and operated by my boyhood friend, Byron Wright. This *Prosperity* was the second of three vessels that Byron owned. The first was the old *Invercan III*, a sixty-foot (eighteen-metre) wooden seiner. The second boat, *Prosperity*, was an aluminum double-decker with all the hydraulic power and equipment to make it a highly efficient fishing machine. Also, it was supplemented with a powerful power skiff. Byron always had to have the most modern and most powerful equipment available. Coupled with his drive to catch more fish than everyone else, this fact made the appearance of the *Prosperity* on the fishing grounds a force that everyone had to recognize. Not always to their liking. In effect, we fished as though we had no friends, which was only partially true. More on that later.

By 1987, a number of conventions had emerged surrounding how you fished the Blue Line. First, there were lineups and a certain protocol for "calling a turn," or determining the order in which boats set their nets. There were only so many setting spots on the Blue Line. Each net covered a quarter of a mile (half a kilometre) when it was open and most of the fish came in close to shore, so there were sometimes eight or ten vessels lined up at a setting spot. The Blue Line was by convention divided into spots related to depth, measured in fathoms. Much of it was conveniently five fathoms deeper each quarter mile so that the prime fishing spot was the sixty-five-fathom spot; inside it was the sixty-fathom spot and outside, of course, was called the seventy-fathom spot. This continued out to about eighty fathoms depth, where few boats fished.

Here was the procedure: the first boat to the Blue Line called his spot, usually the sixty-five-fathom spot, the next vessel would probably take the seventy or sixty spot and others would take spots outside of those already there. They could take a gamble and call the number two place and be in line at sixty-five fathoms or other nearby depths. When the process was complete there would be perhaps eight lineups on the Blue Line, separated by a quarter mile, with five or six vessels in each lineup. As more boats arrived on the grounds a second line behind the Blue Line would form and even a third line and so on all the way east to Sheringham Light, many miles away. Calling a turn had a convention: the last vessel "gave away the turn" to the next. It was done on the radio this way: "Who's last in seventy fathoms?" "Me, the *Progressor.*" "Okay, I'm after you, *Western Prince* last in seventy." The *Western Prince* now had his position in the lineup and would give away the turn to the next vessel wanting to fish that spot.

We never went into that process unprepared. First, we prepared the wheelhouse. On a white board we wrote down the tide and current times. Then we noted the secret radio channels for the few vessels we exchanged information with. Next I set a large piece of white paper on the chart table and marked off the various spots as fifty fathoms, fifty-five, sixty, sixty-five, seventy and so forth. I left a space on each side for information about lines that would form up later in the day: in the shallows at thirty fathoms or so and in the deep at eighty-five fathoms or so. Then I set up the names of the vessels in the various depths. In a way, we now knew the actors in the drama that would unfold. The purpose was to keep track of all the vessels and the lineups.

By watching with binoculars and listening to radio traffic it was possible to get a sense of where the fish were, who was getting them and where they might be headed. This was important, as there were three strategies we could adopt. The first was to stay in the sixty-five- or seventy-fathom spots, but the lineups were long and you waited hours for a set. In a twelve-hour opening fishing time was important. Second, if we didn't want to stay in the six-ty-five-fathom area, we could go to the deep, eighty fathoms or

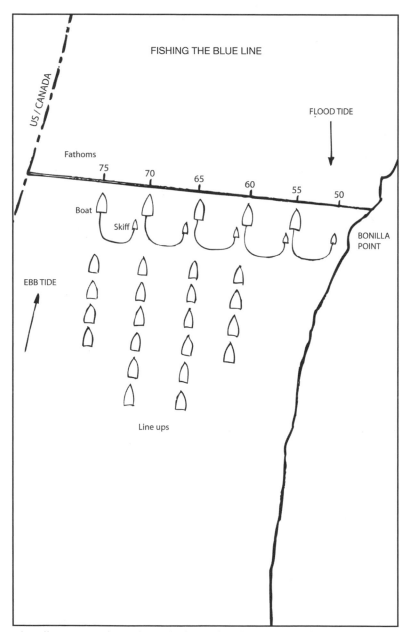

FISHING THE BLUE LINE

This illustration shows how the boats lined up on the Blue Line and waited their turn. With a hundred vessels sometimes scrambling for position, it was chaos. Such lineups are no more, with today's vessel quotas.

more, which had shorter lineups (sometimes none) but usually fewer fish and late in the day, dogfish. Third, we could go to the shallows, but that strategy had its constraints too. The tidal current usually ebbed towards Japan, on most of the tides. But on a good flood the current would flow in the opposite direction towards Sheringham Light. This current was important to watch. We once had snagged our net and left a lead line on the bottom by fishing the shallows on the ebb tide. By setting our net just a little too early, we watched our cork line sink and then re-emerge as the lead line was ripped off the net. A lost day's fishing and embarrassment. Ouch! So it was necessary to wait for the flood before attempting the shallows. Later we came up with a good method of figuring out when it was safe. That is, when the current was flooding the right way. We could then more safely set in the shallows. It was always a gamble, but we knew the risk and took it.

In 1990 Byron launched his third boat, the second aluminum *Prosperity*. This vessel incorporated all that he wanted in a fish boat. Everything was the best and most powerful. For example, we had a double hydraulics system so that if the auxiliary engine broke down we could run the hydraulics off the main. Most vessels had a bow thruster for extra control; we had a bow thruster *and* a stern thruster, both extra powerful, and they could turn the *Prosperity* in its own length. Next we had a powerful skiff named *Brutus* with more power in it than many small seiners. This was important for towing the net, as I will describe.

Let me be frank: we bent the rules wherever possible. Some

FOLLOWING PAGE: The *Prosperity* with a set on three hundred tons of herring. Upon close examination, it's clear that this was a good-looking set, done properly, as all the knots in the web are even. COURTESY THE ESTATE OF BYRON WRIGHT

rules were formal, like the Fisheries Act, and others were the accepted conventions in fishing. First, our net was illegal. We had an extra thirty fathoms (about sixty-two metres) in length. It also had a heavier-than-normal lead line (legal) so our net fished wider, from the length, and perhaps deeper than others. This is where the power in *Brutus* became important. With the extra length of net and *Brutus*'s power, we could "hold our shape" of the net longer than other vessels. Their seines gradually got turned a little, partially closing the open part of the net, as their power skiff could not maintain the maximum fishing shape of the net. We fished more water longer by being "open" longer, even though technically we towed for the same amount of time as the others. We could also close up our net quicker without lifting our lead line (we were always fishing deep with an extra-heavy lead line). The result was that we expected, and usually caught, 10 to 20 percent more fish than other vessels in similar circumstances. *Brutus* and the extra thirty fathoms of a heavy net did their work.

Our net was a far cry from the puny three-and-a-half-strip net we had on the *Jean W* in 1953. Our west coast seine was an "8.75," meaning eight strips of hundred-mesh four-inch web and fifty meshes of six-inch lead line plus twenty-five meshes of cork line border. To support the net we had hundreds of plastic floats, still called corks, but no individual leads threaded onto the lead line. Our west coast seine lead line had the lead *inside* the polyester braided line. It was heavy, at about twenty pounds a foot. Being made of synthetics, the net was strong and did not have to be stripped apart each season. Once made, it was good for years and only required minimal maintenance.

We also bent the rules and conventions of fishing the Blue Line. One convention was that you could not call a turn for your next set unless you had your fish aboard, the "bag over the stern," and you had to be *on* the spot to call the turn, or line up, for that

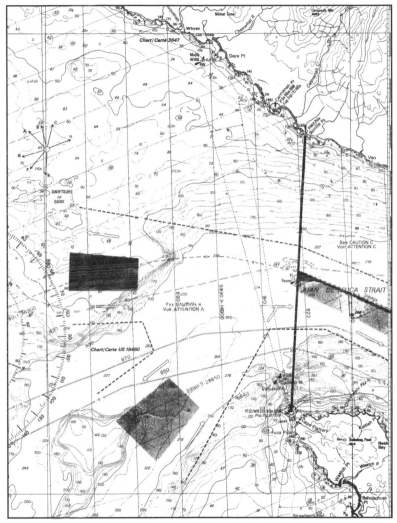

The Bonilla–Tatoosh fishing boundary, commonly known as the Blue
Line. Most of the fish come to the Canadian side of the international
boundary. REPRODUCED WITH THE PERMISSION OF THE CANADIAN HYDROGRAPHIC
SERVICE. NOT TO BE USED FOR NAVIGATION.

particular depth. We violated both rules, not too often, but when necessary. By knowing who was who in the lineups we could call a turn in a selected spot from a mile away. Sometimes the radio would buzz with, "Where the hell is the *Prosperity?* He called sixty-five and he's not here in sixty-five." We would say we were coming or we were close. No one ever called our bluff but I am sure many knew what we were doing and were upset. The point here is that we were well prepared and determined to maximize our performance. And we did. In 1990 we had one delivery of 185,000 pounds of sockeye, 37,000 fish. Mind you, it took us two days.

On a typical day in a typical season we anchored up on the Blue Line close to shore. We had a nice little anchorage, and I marked it on the electronic plotter. It was a little hole where we would not lose our anchor, as many did. The bad bottom there ate anchors. All the spots on the Blue Line for the next day were called and entered on my big sheet and about five a.m. we pulled the hook after our coffee and toast. This morning "mug up" started our day; our full hearty breakfast came later. All the boats assembled into their spots and at six a.m. the DFO (Department of Fisheries and Oceans) patrol vessel announced the opening. Now for twelve hours of stress. We tried to be as fast as possible getting our net back after the first set so we could call our second turn in sixty-five fathoms or wherever before other vessels. Set number two would proceed and we would listen to the radio chatter as vessels jockeyed for position and lineups were created. Imagine my problem, a hundred vessels all cryptically calling turns and there I am trying to get the information down on paper. "*Sunrise* after Teddy in seventy" meant the *Pacific Sunrise* was after a vessel skippered by Teddy—who was he? Were there lots of fish in seventy fathoms of depth? Don't know. "*Challenger* giving up seventy-five and after Pete in eighty-five." No fish for him in seventy-five? No, he felt the lineup was too long, at five boats, with only three boats in line in eighty-five fathoms. I'd keep the glasses on those in at eighty-five, we might want to leave sixty-five fathoms and go there, as our lineup was also five boats. If the boats ahead of us in our line in sixty-five fathoms got few fish and we saw good catches in eighty-five, we moved. And so it went. It was managed chaos. Boats came and went and the worst were the line-jumpers. They would call a turn on say seventy fathoms and then move to sixty fathoms. They were adjusting their strategy and I had to keep track of the radio conversations of dozens of boats calling turns and changing lineups. The big sheet of paper on the chart table told us everything.

We always monitored the vessels fishing the deep but seldom went there. The logs record the sad story. "Nothing here, 100 pinks, 25 sockeye, wrong move." "Nothing in 90, too many dogfish, late." We often had tried to squeeze in an extra set late in the day and ran out to the deep. But we didn't have much success, as I recall, and the logs bear me out. Keeping a record of each set and a commentary was useful, as we had the history of each season. But our favourite strategy was heading for the shallows, in spite of our lost lead line, lying mute on the bottom. No one wanted to be the first in the shallows because if you were too early you could lose your lead line like we did, so everyone waited till they saw a set in the shallows that was trouble-free, meaning the current was flooding. We could predict it accurately by then. The second aluminum *Prosperity* had a temperature gauge in its hull. When the flood started it brought a surge of warmer water with it from the gyre on "Big Bank" (La Perouse Bank). The temperature would jump just like that and we immediately headed for the shallows and set.

If we were fast and lucky we could get two or three sets in before we had competition. And sometimes the surge brought lots of fish to the shallows. My role was simple: keep an ear to the radio and use the glasses to monitor fishing activity. When every set was over and Byron came into the wheelhouse I could give him a more or less complete picture of fishing activity on the Blue Line. Few other vessels were as organized as we were and had the equipment to take advantage of all the opportunities that arose. And we had an attitude, too.

Our attitude was that we were the best, and we wanted to control as much of our fishing as possible. Prior to our set in a lineup we would line everybody up in the following fashion. If we were to set in sixty-five fathoms we contacted the boats setting to the inside (sixty fathoms) and outside (seventy fathoms) of us. We would never set behind anyone, as some boats did. The boat before us would have closed his net and the ebb would carry him towards the Blue Line. It would be easy to set behind him, as his net was not fishing. But our purpose was to maximize our opportunities. So we called the boat on the inside and asked him to set and we would set our skiff off his bow. We then set and asked the boat outside of us to set and drop his skiff on our bow. Everyone liked this approach as there was no chance of "cutting someone off" by setting in front of him. It was neat and tidy. The quarter- mile (half-kilometre) ring on the radar was ideal for calculating your distance from the other boats setting. We wanted this orderly procedure because with our extra thirty fathoms of net we needed as much room as possible. We generally covered the accepted expanse of water like the others but our longer net had a bigger bight in it. That is, the arc of our net was bigger than others, but it was just a quarter-mile (half-kilometre) open in the front like the others. To maximize our set we had to get it positioned the way we wanted. To the outside observer we were merely being our aggressive selves but we had a deeper purpose: to maximize the fishing time with our bigger net.

What was it like overall, on the Blue Line? Well, it was stressful and sometimes chaotic. But we had a clear purpose: to be the best. And over time, we logged enough evidence to show that we were definitely up there. I actually kept several logbooks, one for Byron in the pilothouse, one for his and my records, the big black book for the boat and my own personal log. Here is one day on the Blue Line, according to my logs:

## LOGBOOK FV *PROSPERITY*
### August 25,1991
### "Blue line"

**Current:**

| Turns: | Maximum | Velocity |
|---|---|---|
| 00:35 | 02:15 | +0.4 knots |
| 03:55 | 08:15 | -1.7 knots |
| 12:10 | 14:35 | +0.8 knots |
| 17:00 | 20:50 | -1.6 knots |

Note: add towing speed on Ebb tide. Approx. .3 knots
Gives calculation of time to Boundary on Ebb.


**Set 1:** Number 2 in 65 fathom line, temperature 53 degrees F.
Time 6:20
Open: 16 minutes
Time to close- up: 14 minutes
Fish: 1,200 sockeye
Comment: Best spot

**Set 2:** In 65 fathom line, temperature 53 degrees F.
Time 7:59
Open: 13 minutes
Time to close- up: 14 minutes

Fish: 250 sockeye
Comment: Move to 60 fathoms, too many boats in line-up.

**Set 3:** In 60 fathom line, temperature 53 degrees F.
Time 9:23
Open: 14 minutes
Time to close- up: 15 minutes
Fish: 600 sockeye
Comment: strong ebb tide

**Set 4:** In 55 fathom line, temperature 53 degrees F.
Time 11:05
Open: 16 minutes
Time to close- up: 14 minutes
Fish: 100 sockeye
Comment: still ebbing, move to shallows on flood

**Set 5:** In 38-46 fathoms! Start of flood. No boats!
Time 13:46
Open: 12 minutes
Time to close- up: 24 minutes
Fish: 1,500 sockeye!!!

CHAPTER TWELVE

# THE US-CANADA FISH WAR

In 1997 we were in a "fish war" with the US. The dispute was over salmon, as usual. While the details are important and complex, the key point was that Canada, in response to perceived US intransigence, developed a "Canada-first fishing strategy." In simple terms the decision meant that Canada was not bound by any previous agreement with the US to manage fisheries in a way that would ensure the US received its share of salmon, as had been the case under various earlier agreements.

Fish do not respect national boundaries, so salmon returning to the Fraser River might cross the Canada–Alaska boundary and cross the Canada–US boundary again in Juan de Fuca Strait and Puget Sound. Who gets what had to be negotiated to ensure good management of the stocks. Other frictions arose, of course. For example, the US had a big coho salmon hatchery program but the coho came into Canadian waters and the Canadian trollers had a field day on the US-bound fish. The two countries had set up a mechanism to resolve such disputes with the International Pacific Salmon Commission, and our cooperation had a long history: way back, the US had financed the fishways in the Fraser Canyon at Hell's Gate after the disastrous slides of 1913–14.

The current conflict was over sharing the catch. Canada wanted to stop the interception of sockeye salmon by the Alaskans (the so-called "Noyes Island" fishery) and the US wanted the Canadian troll fishery on American coho to stop. Agreement was difficult because it pitted various groups of fishermen against each other. Why should the Canadian trollers make a sacrifice to benefit the seine and gillnet fishermen? Why should the Alaskan fishermen make a sacrifice to benefit "lower 48" fishermen? These intractable issues brought about a small fish war.

Understandably, Canada wanted to put pressure on the US. One possible Canadian strategy was to send the fleet to Juan de Fuca (the Blue Line) and catch all the fish. No agreement, no share. So we fishermen were coerced into the fish war. The battle moved from hotel meeting rooms to the high seas.

The new Canadian fishing strategy allowed the salmon fleet that fished the Blue Line (the Bonilla–Tatoosh boundary) an open season. In effect, you could fish as much as you wanted. Canadian officials felt this strategy would put significant pressure on Washington state fishermen by taking all the fish that might enter Puget Sound and other US waters. Denying their boats fish might once again bring the US to the bargaining table, as it had in the past during the fight over pink salmon.

The strategy was seen as a good one in that the fishing fleet cooperated and fished the Blue Line intensively. Unfortunately there were very few fish, and accordingly very few vessels fished the Blue Line during the so-called fish war. But we on the *Prosperity* were there. And the fishing was lousy. But we did have one set that in retrospect had some interesting—or maybe just comic—elements to it.

Our normal Blue Line strategy involved fishing a set at the best depth, sixty-five fathoms, and then moving into shallow water when the flood came, bringing the fish to the thirty-fathom depth. As I mentioned, you could not normally fish there on the ebb tide because you hooked up, and we had lost that much-lamented lead line there. You always had to be cautious, and other boats usually waited until we set to be sure that the tide was all right for them. Timing was important and our key indicator for the flood current was the quick rise in temperature, a degree or so, around the time the flood should come. It varied depending upon the size of the tides.

On the day in question fog was heavy and we left the sixty-five-fathom setting depth as there were too many boats ahead of us and fishing was, as I said, lousy overall. We lay in the shallows waiting for the temperature rise to signal the flood tide. Suddenly, the ocean temperature shot up and I told Byron. He put the clutch in gear and said, "Where are we?" I said we were in thirty-five fathoms and half a mile (just under a kilometre) over the boundary. In effect, in illegal territory. "That thing is haywire," he said, and then blew the horn to set the net. I think his statement was somehow for my consumption as the radar did not lie. In any event we were towing on our set, well over the Blue Line boundary, when the fog suddenly lifted and we could see the whole fleet. And they could see us.

Soon the chatter started on the fishing radio channel. "What the hell is the *Prosperity* doing?"

"Christ, he's way over the line."

"Why doesn't DFO do something about that bastard?"

"He hasn't bent the boundary, he's broken it."

And so on and on. One or two incurred Byron's wrath from age-old disputes and strong words were exchanged between them. All this radio chatter as we were towing reached the ears of the DFO fish cops and they had to do something. But what? We were in a fish war and were supposed to catch all the fish available, to make the Americans mad. Perhaps arresting some of the soldiers in the war (us) would defeat the purpose of the Canadian strategy. One possible move by the DFO would be to say nothing about our indiscretion. But it was not to be so. The DFO fish cops were soon alongside the *Prosperity* in their Zodiac. See what they want, said Byron. I stepped out of the pilothouse and leaned over the side and they asked: You the skipper? No, I replied. Ask him to talk to us. So Byron did.

"You are one-quarter of a mile over the line," they said.

"I am not fishing," Byron said. This was too far-fetched. We were towing on one end of the net and our skiff, *Brutus*, was towing on the other end. What could it be other than fishing?

"I am just positioning my net to put it on the boundary," said Byron, "and I will do so now."

The fisheries officers were as astounded as I was. They looked at each other and incredibly said nothing. So we turned the *Prosperity* around and got the skiff to do the same and towed the net back to the boundary. This of course was watched by the fleet and they gave us the hoo-ha on the airwaves:

"Looks like the *Prosperity* is fishing for the fish going back."

"Maybe Byron better check his radar, he's going the wrong way."

"This is the damndest set I've ever seen out here."

"This is a strange way to fight the fish war."

There was much more. We paid them no mind, made our set and pursed up and drummed the net back on board. However, all the hard towing had ripped the net. We had a nice straight 150-fathom rip in the third strip of web. So we went into Port Renfrew, back-hauled the net and laced up the rip. We were ready again to play our role in the fish war.

Now, many years later, I have puzzled it all out. Byron knew we were over the boundary but the bottom was better there and the chance of snagging our net was minimal. Second, it was foggy as hell and maybe the fish cops, several miles away, were not monitoring their radar or the radio. And third, we were in a fish war. Byron's claim that we were not fishing was outrageous but by saying he was "positioning" his net he gave the DFO fish cops a way to say they had forced Byron to get behind the boundary. And therefore there was no unnecessary paperwork, I assume. They were the true diplomats in the fish war. As for us, it was just another day on the Blue Line in the fish war of 1997. The fish war ended with an agreement but it was a harbinger of things to come. The war then moved from the fishing grounds back to the meeting rooms. New Canada–US agreements were worked out, but they had little effect on us. And we never received any medals for our role.

## CHAPTER THIRTEEN

# Fishing Roe Herring
# in the Foote Islands

After the collapse of the herring fishery in the 1960s, in which I'd played some part, there was no herring fishery on the coast for several decades. It wasn't until the late 1980s and early 1990s that the herring stocks started to rebound, and once there was a healthy fishery I fished herring with Byron Wright on the *Prosperity*. The skills and equipment we used in fishing for salmon were transferable to the herring fishery. We had a special seine for herring but the same power skiff, *Brutus*, and the same crew. But it was different in some ways and we made the necessary adjustments. Having refrigerated sea water (RSW) for our tanks meant we could preserve our quality and demand a premium for that quality.

One big change was that after the collapse of the initial herring fishery there was no longer a fishmeal reduction fishery. Only a small food herring operation was allowed. However, when the stocks rebounded a new fishery emerged producing a (short-lived) bonanza for fishermen. So by the 1980s fishermen were making sets of fish worth a million dollars. From the measly $20 per ton I received in the 1960s herring reduction fishery, fishermen were receiving up to $3,500 per ton! It was not the fish that were valuable, however; it was the roe, the eggs. The Japanese herring fishery had collapsed and there was a new demand in Japan for herring roe from BC. Among other things, the roe was part of the Japanese New Year's gift-giving custom. It was highly prized. And we had it.

It took a number of years to bring some sort of order into the fishery. First, the Japanese buyers competed with each other and usually outbid a rational price, which was to the benefit of BC fishermen. The Japanese decided to get organized and sort out the prices between the importers of the roe and the distributors of the roe. So in Japan they formed a number of cartels to control the product and they were able to stabilize the prices and set up import quotas to ensure everyone, or almost everyone, made a profit, even if it was small. Next, BC fishermen and the DFO had to bring some sort of order to the fishery. The old "Klondike" approach—a mad rush to set your net before the fishery was closed—had to be eliminated. Some fisheries were only fifteen minutes! Next, the number of licenses was fixed and fixed quotas were assigned to those vessels. As a result, it became an orderly fishery. While we also fished the west coast of Vancouver Island and the Gulf of Georgia, the central coast was our favourite locale for fishing roe herring.

The Foote Islands are in Spiller Channel, on the central coast, and were a special herring spawning area. The herring came into the various inlets and schooled up prior to spawning. In the meantime, the herring fleet anchored up and waited until the

---

FOLLOWING PAGE: The arrows here show the route of the herring in and out of the little pass behind the Foote Islets where we caught them. They were tricky to catch because our sonar was useless in that shallow, uneven fishing ground. REPRODUCED WITH THE PERMISSION OF THE CANADIAN HYDROGRAPHIC SERVICE. NOT TO BE USED FOR NAVIGATION.

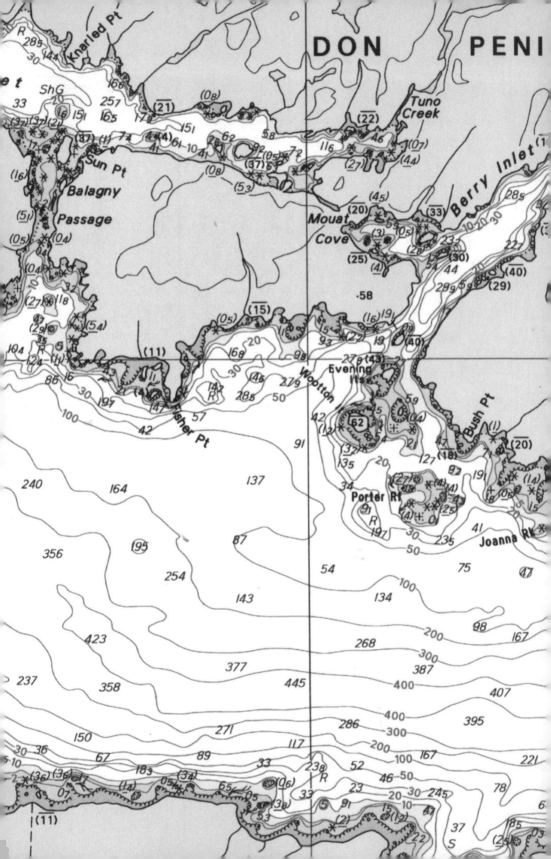

herring matured and the egg sac grew large and was of the right size for the market. Test boats would set on the fish and sample them to measure the roe content. The ideal roe content was about 13 percent of the total weight. So as the test boats fished they announced the roe percentage each day. It increased at varying rates. The plan was to get the maximum percentage we could, but if we waited too long the fish would spawn and then we'd make no money. Spawned-out fish had no value. So it was an anxious time. When was the right time to open the fishery? Too soon and the roe content was low, too late and no roe at all. You could only wait.

The opening of the fishery was determined by the DFO and the various fishing companies. The companies organized their fishermen into pools of eight vessels with a "pool captain" responsible for organizing his pool. The purpose of this set-up was to control the fishing sets and thus to control the catch, ensuring it was within the quota set by the DFO. The pool captains met with the DFO manager and reviewed the test boat data and other information. Upon some sort of an agreement the fleet was placed on twenty-four-hour stand-by and the fishery would open subject to last-minute test results. At the appointed time the fishery was open. But Spiller Channel was thirty miles (fifty kilometres) long and the fish were moving about. It was necessary to find them. Because the fish moved up and down the channel they would often go through the little pass behind the Foote Islands. But it was a tricky place to fish for a number of reasons.

As you can see on the chart on pages 184–85, the setting spot in the pass has lots of shallow water and rocks—an "itchy

PREVIOUS PAGE: During the fabled fifteen-minute herring roe fishery openings in Barkley Sound, countless boats would scramble for position. Today, each set of the net is controlled and quotas are strictly adhered to. BRIAN GAUVIN 2007

bottom," as we say. Also, the pass was narrow, so it was not possible to "swing your whole net," meaning you had to make a long narrow set or even a short set, not using all of your net. The standard net was about 225 fathoms long. In addition to these geographical factors affecting how you set your net, there was another problem. The fish were hard to see, and this was due to the peculiarities of the area, the fish behaviour and how sonar works. We would enter the pass with our radios on, our sounders operating and our sonars sweeping the area around the vessel. We had two sonars, one broad beam and one narrow beam for searching.

A big set of herring during the reduction fishery in the 1950s would require other boats to come in and help pull up the net, as seen here. Back then, before the devastation of the fishery, you could make sets of 300 to 350 tons. COURTESY ALAN HAIG-BROWN

The brailers we used to scoop herring from our seines were soon replaced with hydraulic pumps. Pumping was effective for herring and sardine catches. BRIAN GAUVIN 2007

Herring in a purse seine, during a 1989 opening in Barkley Sound. Fishing times were short and the herring were in tight schools, resulting in a crowded fishing ground. BRIAN GAUVIN 2007

The sounders only showed the fish when we were directly over them, so we needed the sonars to find the fish. Unfortunately, the sonar was only marginally useful there. It would find the herring, that is, show them on the screen, only after or before they entered the pass. We had to guess if they were coming or going. Either way it was usually too late, as they were fast-moving fish. We couldn't find the fish when they were *in* the pass because the sonar bounced off the cliffs on the shore side and also gave mixed signals from the small islands on the seaward side. The result was just a sea of red on the sonar, meaning the signal was bouncing off the underwater cliffs and the little islands. No sign of fish as their signal, if any, was mixed with that of everything else.

From my point of view in the pilothouse, when the sonar swept and showed nothing but red on the screen, it had hit cliffs on the shore or the islands outside of us. Even using the tilt to scan different depths of the signal was no help. If the fish were coming through the pass and next to the cliffs they were just more red blotches on the sonar screen. I was, in effect, blind. Ultimately the result was that we could never tell for sure when the herring were there. Sometimes we would set, thinking they might be coming into the pass, then we would find out they were going the other way. Or vice versa. Frustrating.

We did solve the problem, and here is how we did it. We were working with our pool partners and they were monitoring the fish, just like us. They kept us informed as to what they thought the herring were doing in the pass and outside of it. We got set up as best we could to get them. We were in the Bella Coola pool and one of our partners was the FV *Vicious Fisher*. He lay inside us and had his sonars working also. We told our manager that we

PREVIOUS PAGE: After a big set in Barkley Sound in 2004, the crewmen on this seiner are drying up the net so they can pump the last of the herring into their hold. BRIAN GAUVIN

were going to set and he contacted the DFO to get final approval. (DFO officials were controlling all the pools and determining the sets.) Working closely with the *Vicious Fisher* we were sure the fish had come into the pass and the red on our screen might be fish and not a rock bluff. We had already made two sets that day and caught nothing. We made a trial run of our proposed set, as we did not want to drop our net on a rock pile. When we were

Herring were first salted for food, then caught for reduction into meal and oil, then caught for their roe. Now, a small food herring fishery also exists. CITY OF RICHMOND ARCHIVES PHOTOGRAPH #1985 4 510

ready we set our net close to the beach and the *Vicious Fisher* went ahead of us very slowly and called the depth. He was ensuring that we were setting in good bottom. We followed in his wake. That way we knew we were not dropping our net in a bad place.

Our set of the net was a "banana," long and skinny, not the usual nice circle. We were in a narrow spot and the power skiff on the beach end of the net had his bow right up tight to the cliff face. This was part of the plan as it was deep there and when we pursed our net it would pull us and our net up and away from the shallow spots outside of us that contained the danger. That is, the bag (or bight) of our net was away from the boat and out in the shallow places, and we were pursing the boat and the net into the deeper part. Or so we hoped. It was a tense moment: would our net be clear of the rock piles and would we have the fish? Yes, and yes, and as we pursed our net we saw several herring dropping out of the net as we drummed aboard the first part of the net. How much we had we didn't know as our sonar was useless. (Usually the sonar could indicate quite accurately how much was in the net.)

As we pursed up we could see the cork line start to sink, meaning lots of fish. We put the *Vicious Fisher* on our cork line and slowly pursed up. Once we had the purse rings up and on the iron bar (the "ring stripper") we had to dry up the net prior to pumping the fish. We used a hydraulic pump lowered into the net rather than brailing because of the large amount of fish. This was also a tricky business. If you had lots of fish and drying up wasn't done right you could split your net and lose them all. The mantra was "keep the knots even," meaning distribute the strain evenly throughout the net. By looking at how the net hung as we dried up we could see the shape of the knots. Straight up and down meshes and all aligned was what we wanted. Sometimes even on a small set of fifty tons the fish are heavy and great care must be taken. Once, on big set in the Gulf of Georgia, our net started to split as we lifted the fish up. The rip was straight up and down on the web we were drying up. But it was closed, held together by the strain on the net. A hole was there but the fish couldn't get out. We stopped drying up, took a lead ball of about ten pounds, attached a line and dropped it into the net. When it hit the fish we pulled it up and measured the depth. We needed 110 feet (33 metres) of hose to get to the fish so we attached every piece of hose we had and lowered the pump into the net. At first there were not many fish as they were not tightly packed, but after pumping for an hour we nervously dried up the net some more, expecting it to split at any moment. The pump rewarded us by eventually pumping lots of fish into our hatch. Success!

In the Foote Islands we did get our big set, about three hundred tons. So we loaded the *Vicious Fisher* with about a hundred tons and he left for Prince Rupert. We then loaded our packer, the *Pacific Horizon*, with a hundred tons. And then ourselves, about eighty tons, and the rest we gave away to a boat in our pool. We were loaded to the gunnels. This meant we had little freeboard (the boat was very low in the water, and our decks awash) so we had to be sure the scuppers were open so water could drain off. We had made a successful set in the Foote Islands.

The trip south was not uneventful. We anchored behind Addenbrooke Island waiting for better weather before we crossed Queen Charlotte Sound. We wanted to wait for the wind to go down and hoped that with the ebb tide and the southeast wind both going in the same direction the swells would be smaller. Cape Caution got its name for a reason. In the morning when it was time to leave we tried to pull up the anchor. No luck—it was glued to the bottom. The captain tried the usual tricks, such as trying to pull from different angles and speeding up the engine to ensure full power to the hydraulic pumps, all to no avail. One last desperate measure was required. We paid out all of the anchor line by backing up so that nothing but a few turns of the cable were left on the anchor winch. Then the boat went ahead at full speed until the line was tight. The bow went down about a fathom and then bang! Something broke below us as the anchor line went slack. Up came just the chain and the shank of the anchor. The flukes had broken off.

We were free but now had a new problem. We had to cross Queen Charlotte Sound in very foul weather (March) and without an anchor our insurance would be invalid. Time to get out the spare anchor. We did, and after much jury-rigging got the six hundred pounds of anchor from the deck to the anchor chock. On our way again, we said goodbye to the Foote Islands and the herring roe fishery for that season.

## CHAPTER FOURTEEN

# SARDINES COME TO BC

In the late 1990s, sardines (*Sardinops sagax*) returned to the coast of BC after an absence of fifty years. The previous fishery lasted from around 1922 to about 1945. The catches were large, up to forty thousand tons in a year. Almost all of the fish went to reduction plants for fishmeal and oil. However, a small amount of the catch was canned into one-pound cans and sold as "pilchards," which is also a common name for sardines. I even ate them back when they were for sale in the BC Packers store in Alert Bay in the 1940s. That fishery collapsed, however, probably due to environmental conditions, but the decline was surely hastened by the fishing of the spawning stocks in California. (Few sardines spawned in BC.) Then, in 1997, Richard Leo was fishing for herring on the FV *Wamalo Sea* in Kyoquot Sound and caught sixty tons of sardines. After much soul-searching and bureaucratic gyrations by the Department of Fisheries and Oceans, the sardine fishery was launched.

The fishery proceeded in three stages: first there was an "exploratory fishery," then it became an "experimental fishery" and finally it became a "commercial fishery." The point of this procedure was to ensure that there were sufficient stocks to sustain a

199

This chart shows the various places we looked for sardines in Kyoqout Sound. We found them at last in Amai Inlet. It was a long way to go for sardines. REPRODUCED WITH THE PERMISSION OF THE CANADIAN HYDROGRAPHIC SERVICE. NOT TO BE USED FOR NAVIGATION.

fishery. Incredibly, this process took ten years! The millstones of the DFO bureaucracy grind exceedingly fine. In the meantime, US fishermen in Washington and Oregon had developed a fishery of over 40,000 tons per year over the same time period. As the Canadian fishery developed, more and more licenses were issued, culminating in twenty-five commercial licenses and twenty-five communal commercial licenses issued to First Nations bands. The final management plan set the annual quota and it was divided equally among all the licensees. And each individual quota could be transferred to another vessel so it was possible for one vessel to fish up to five licenses at one time, which made the fishery economically viable for a vessel.

Sardines have been extensively studied for over fifty years. With the collapse of the stocks in the 1940s, the California and US governments established the California Cooperative Fisheries Investigation (CalCOFI) program, which was charged with doing scientific research on sardines. The biology of sardines is by now well understood, although predicting their abundance is difficult. It is clear that they spawn off California in the spring and after a year or so they begin to migrate up the coast to Washington, Oregon and BC. After a summer of feeding in BC they head back to California in late autumn. That is the general pattern for sardines but it varies depending upon environmental conditions such as water temperature, which is linked to their food.

From the point of view of a BC sardine fisherman, the sardines usually appear on our coast after ocean temperatures rise to about twelve degrees Celsius. They will be about 140 grams in size at first in BC and their weight will increase over the summer as they feed. Older year-classes (each group of new recruits is assigned a year) may contain fish that are larger than younger year-classes, so that larger sardines of 190 grams are caught in some years. At first, they show offshore and are seen by the hake draggers. Then they start to flood into the various inlets looking to feed. If food is plentiful they will stay in an inlet until it disappears, at which point they will leave the inlet and continue their search in another. When trying to find sardines, fishermen first check all the inlets, where they are easier to catch and it is a safer environment for fishing. Offshore fishing is always fraught with danger so only the larger vessels can fish there. We tried fishing offshore but on one occasion our skiff's painter broke and the safety strap pulled the skiff sideways and it swamped. Back to the safety of the inlets for us. In recent years more and more fish have been taken offshore.

In the early years of sardine fishing it was difficult to find them, as we didn't know their behaviour. And at the time only a small number of vessels fished them—at first only seven, "The Magnificent Seven," so-called because there were only seven licenses at first. As one of the seven, the procedure for the *Prosperity* was to leave Steveston and head for the Johnstone Straits, hoping for an easy fishery in inside waters. So we would check Beaver Cove, Port Hardy and all the little coves around the inside tip of Vancouver Island. We generally tried to avoid crossing Queen Charlotte Sound to fish in Fitz Hugh Sound and other inlets as we were conscious of fuel costs. Travelling 300 miles (480 kilometres) to catch fish and then running back the same distance for a delivery made costs prohibitive. If there was nothing for us on the inside of Vancouver Island we headed around Cape Scott and checked the "outside" inlets, starting with Quatsino Sound. We usually had good luck there, and Quatsino Narrows was a favourite spot. Sardines would go through the narrows into Holberg Inlet on the flood tide and out again on the ebb. We could catch them either way as the narrows concentrated the various small schools into a large body of fish. We called them "commuters" because their behaviour was predictable, governed by the tide.

This logbook entry records us leaving Steveston, going around Cape Scott and looking for sardines in Quatsino Sound. We then moved on to Kyoquot Sound, and in Amai Inlet we made several sets to get a load of sardines. As can be seen on the pages, we always recorded water temperatures. DON PEPPER

If there was nothing in Quatsino we would proceed to the next inlet, maybe Kyuquot Sound. We were always searching. You found sardines by watching for signs of sea life—birds were one indicator, and in later years humpback whales fed on them, so if you found the whales you found the fish. Failing birds or whales, good eyesight was the criterion for success. Sardines barely showed on the surface of the water. We called them "breezers," as they looked like a small dark breeze on the water. Once you were close you could distinguish them from immature herring. We could also test the size of the fish by casting a herring jig with many hooks amongst them and getting a sample of the school.

Estimating the size of the schools before we set our net was also a problem. As sardines were more or less surface feeders, the sounder was of no use. When you went over the school they dispersed in front of the boat so the sounder showed nothing but you could actually see the fish on each side of the boat. Weird! The only reliable indicator was the sonar. After a while our experience in sonar operation in the herring roe fishery paid off and we became proficient in estimating the size of schools. The *Prosperity* could comfortably carry eighty-two tons so we knew how many fish we wanted. After a few years of learning about their behaviour we were better able to plan our fishery.

Finding sardines was difficult at first, but once that problem was solved catching them was easy. We used our herring seine and usually made a round set around a school. Occasionally we made a tow set if they were travelling down an inlet. In any event, setting on sardines was much like setting on herring. They were fairly easy to handle, although sometimes they were "heavy," or difficult to dry up in the net. But mostly they were easy to catch and pump with a fish pump or, alternatively, brail aboard. As sardines are delicate we preferred to brail to preserve the quality, but later, as we refined our pumping technique, we could pump and not harm the fish.

Sometimes knowledge and experience in fishing can produce a result that is surprising. We fished sardines over the entire coast and had a mental picture of how fishing would be done in each area. In Smith Inlet in the Ahclakerho Basin we knew the fish would be of poor quality and getting through the little narrows would be tricky. In Quatsino we knew that the best strategy for getting fish was to sit at Quatsino Narrows and see if the sardines were to-ing and fro-ing into Holberg Inlet. In Barkley Sound we always wanted to be in Junction Pass at low water slack. In our minds these were strategies that had a high probability of a good payoff. Sometimes we were right in our plans and we were rewarded.

We had fished Amai Inlet in Kyuquot Sound and noticed that sardines went to the head of the inlet at night and at dawn came down the beach on the south side. Knowing this behaviour meant for a nice fishing experience. In planning one fishing trip Byron Wright said to me: "Don, here is what we will do and how it is going to work. We will leave Steveston and be in Amai Inlet about five a.m. We will drop the hook [anchor] for an hour or so, wake up the crew, have some coffee and toast, pull the hook about seven and set the net. The sardines should come marching down the beach at that time and we will be nicely positioned to catch them." So we left Steveston and proceeded to Amai Inlet and arrived at the appointed time. Needless to say, it worked out: the sardines came down the beach, and we made a small open set and let them enter our net. Over the day we got a full load of sardines.

Afterwards Byron commented to me that it had all worked out exactly as planned. He emphasized the word "exactly." I disagreed and said so. Not exactly, I noted. How so? he queried. Well, I said, we had trouble with our 110-volt inverter and the toaster wasn't working in the morning so we did not have toast with our coffee. Things never work out exactly in the fishing racket.

The new sardine fishery demanded new markets, and they were difficult to develop. But ultimately markets were found and sardines supplied to them, although even today the West Coast sardine fishery is a difficult proposition. The BC market is a very small player in a large commodity market and must compete on price and quality. And for a variety of reasons related to economic conditions, principally price, BC fishermen may not always catch all of the quota.

Overall, it was exciting and pleasurable to fish sardines. We could more or less go where we wanted and fish when we wanted, which was so very different from the highly regulated salmon and herring fisheries. Sardines come and go in cycles, though. American researchers found in analyzing nearly two thousand years of data collected from drilled sediment that cycles of abundance and scarcity fluctuated in forty to fifty cycles. On average, you could expect forty years of good sardine fishing, forty years of waiting. So if my arithmetic is correct, watch out around 2030 for the disappearance of sardines from BC waters.

CHAPTER FIFTEEN

# THE LAST VOYAGE
# OF THE *PROSPERITY*

On September 20, 2004, the FV *Prosperity* left Steveston for the fishing grounds of coastal BC. The captain was Byron Wright and he had many of his "old crew" on board. Old in the sense that some of us had fished with him for twenty years, while it was much longer for me. Byron and I had fished together in the 1960s! The species we were after were sardines. We went through Seymour Narrows without an incident and entered the Johnstone Straits—we were taking the "inside" route. So the first stop was Port Hardy for ice and to see if sardines were in Bear Cove or anywhere nearby. No luck. The next decision was obvious, we had to go around Cape Scott and start exploring all the west coast inlets.

This was a different trip that those of previous years. Byron was slowly dying of renal failure and we could only watch him slowly shrink before our eyes. We knew what the end would be. So when he said he wanted to make one more trip we knew it was going to be the last hurrah. Many of our trips over the years had that positive excitement of once more meeting and over-coming the various challenges of catching fish. But this one was something entirely different. We understood, or thought we did, why Byron wanted the trip, but the sadness was still there. We would be going through the motions of our last trip together. We were going fishing with heavy hearts.

Rounding Cape Scott I could see the white beach at Nels Bight, where campers set up their tents and enjoy the wilderness. The ocean was very calm and the sun was shining brightly. Cape Scott is notorious for bad weather because two ocean systems meet there. We were in luck as it was smooth sailing around the cape. We then went into Quatsino Sound to see if there were any sardines. The *Ocean Marauder* was in there but he reported that fish were scarce. Small schools and scattered. However, we explored each of our usual spots to be sure. "You have to know where the fish aren't," said Byron, which was always part of his fishing strategy.

We then went into Holberg Inlet. Quatsino Narrows was where we expected to get sardines as we had so often in the past. We could see the A-frame log dump, where loggers lifted their logs into the water for transport. I know from my hiking experience that people often get lost coming from the Cape Scott trailhead and end up there, and loggers will tell them how to get to the pub in Holberg. So they are no longer lost and have beer to drink. We wouldn't be going to the pub on this trip, though.

As I mentioned, the best way to find sardines in Quatsino Sound is to watch the narrows as the sardines go in and out of Holberg Inlet. They are sort of like commuters, going into the inlet on the flood and leaving on the ebb. They school and wait for the tide in the narrows to push them in and out of the inlet. In previous years we had caught many tons on either side of the narrows by taking advantage of that behaviour. This time we saw only immature herring.

Immature herring can be big trouble if you catch them. First, they may gill in your net from one end to the other and they are a mess to clean out of the net. Also, the Fisheries people will be upset, which is not good. We got excited when we saw many more "flippers" on the surface of the water but they turned out to be immature herring also, so no luck there. More looking around and no sardines. They had left. So we could only head for the next inlets on our itinerary.

The prospect of moving on was not exciting as we had to go around Cape Cook, which usually meant bad weather, but the crossing was calm. Cape Cook is always an itchy spot as you are very exposed because the peninsula sticks out a long way into the broad Pacific. I have had bad experiences off Cape Cook, and the time we went into Sea Otter Cove because of bad weather sticks in my memory. Sick as a dog. Also, my shipmates remembered my seasickness episode and always reminded me of it. My diet of ginger ale and soda crackers helped but was not a total cure. The older you get the more susceptible you are to seasickness. Weird. This time, however, the sea was smooth as silk.

So what happened? Well, we decided not to go into Kyuquot Sound and went right into Esperanza Inlet. We anchored up about midnight in a little bay along with a bunch of other fishing boats. There were trollers out fishing for spring salmon, some long-liners fishing for sharks ("dogfish") and a few gillnetters getting ready for a chum salmon fishery. It was a small community of fishermen in a remote spot.

We were up at five a.m. to pull the hook, have toast and coffee, and look for fish at daylight. We cruised off Centre Island

FOLLOWING PAGE: Launched in 1990, the second aluminum *Prosperity* had everything Byron Wright wanted in a boat. In its first season, we loaded the boat with sockeye fishing the Blue Line in Juan de Fuca Strait. Sold just before Byron's death, the *Prosperity* is still active in the industry, and used mainly to fish herring and sardines. COURTESY THE ESTATE OF BYRON WRIGHT

and we found them. Kim Anderson was the relief skipper on the wheel so he told me to call Byron. It took Byron twenty minutes to come up the stairs to the pilothouse and Kim had to show him where we were and where the fish were. Sad to see. He was really sick. But several schools of sardines were showing on the surface and we could track them on our sonar. Byron set at seven-thirty and it was an easy set as the sardines were "in the bag" (showing in the net) and on the sonar at all times, giving pleasure to Byron and to me. It was a nice feeling; your hopes are not always realized in the fishing life.

So we pursed up, dried up the net and started brailing. Sardines must be handled carefully so we took our time and put them into tanks that had the requisite amount of refrigerated sea water. Kim Anderson worked the brailer handle, Garth Anderson and Larry Benson were on the brailer and I was out of sight on the brailer release. Byron watched from the galley, too weak to come on deck and supervise. No matter, we had done all of this many times before. The brailer efficiently dips fish out of the net and we dipped 165 times. After 100 I was tired, but overall it was easy for us as we were an experienced crew. We got sixty-five tons and filled four tanks—it was "just enough" said Byron. The FV *Prosperity* was fourteen years old and I had fished on it since it was new. Where did the time go? We were all aware that this would be the last trip for the captain and me, as economics and age dictated new vistas. Hey, we'd done everything! We had nothing to prove. Like Alexander the Great, we had conquered all.

We had the fish aboard by noon. So we decided to go with the government's fishery observer into Zeballos. The observer monitored our fishing operations to ensure we obeyed all the rules of our license (too many to mention). He was also going to work at the unloading station, checking the landings of the other sardine boats. He was switching from acting as a certified observer to acting as a government validator. Kind of the same job but one was on the boat, the other on shore. The official noted that there was an excellent restaurant in Zeballos, which was surprising for what was almost a ghost town, and that the waitress was a French-speaking six-foot-tall black beauty who could work, and apparently did, as a high-fashion model. What a strange thing, what brought her here? I asked. The chef was her boyfriend, it seemed, and so good cooking has its benefits.

The FV *Windward Isle* was at the unloading dock and the FV *Star Pacific* had its stern to us. To the right were the *Viking Joy* and the *Kellce Marie*. Other smaller boats were there also. Zeballos has ice and an unloading dock so trucks can transport the fish to plants in Vancouver and elsewhere. Distances are huge in BC so such ports are useful. Zeballos was in the middle of nowhere but did have a hotel, the Zeballos Hotel (we called it "The Zeballos Palace"), which subsequently burnt down, not to mention the great restaurant with the unusual waitress.

Then we headed for home, twenty-six hours away. We would be circumnavigating Vancouver Island, heading down its west coast. We set up the wheel watches and Larry served us a supper of baked chum salmon, as per the captain's request, but we didn't eat it as we were rolling around and seasickness was always a possibility. We went out through Tahsis Inlet to avoid the bad weather we knew was coming and we were anxious to get in front of the weather system.

The barometer ("the glass") was still high and we watched it, because when the barometer falls (the pointer goes down) we know bad weather is coming. We had a two-metre (six-foot) swell behind us and we were going against the tide, so we slowed down. Those conditions produce a big swell. We were also bucking into a southeast wind, so we wanted to get to Estevan Point before it got nasty. Shallow water there makes the ocean much worse, as the swells get bigger. We could do nothing but keep a steady course and hope for no worsening conditions.

We were in luck, as we were able to keep ahead of the bad weather and the wind went down and the tide was in our favour as we cruised along and entered into the Juan de Fuca Strait. This was our old salmon fishing area and we knew it well. We'd had some great catches there but that Blue Line fishery was no more. *Sic transit gloria.* Never mind, those who know, know we were among the best.

We passed several pods of killer whales off Sooke. I took some photos but all my pictures of whales are lousy. Lots of whales come through BC waters these days, more than I remember there being in the past. We saw a humpback whale circling around in Esperanza Inlet as we were fishing. The fisheries officer who came on board said there were three of them. There are also lots of sea lions, seals, sea otters, whales, dolphins and porpoises around now. Next time there is an El Niño we will see even more sea life that is strange to our waters.

Once we reached the calm inside waters we relaxed. Overall the trip had been good in that we got the fish more or less as we planned. It would have been nice if we had found them in Port Hardy but that would have been too good. We needed a little angst to remind us that fishing is a risky business. If it was easy anyone could do it, and we wouldn't be special.

I sensed even then that such special times were slowly passing away as fishing and the world both changed. I no longer fished salmon so that part of my life was over, and I wondered how much longer I would fish sardines. I was not sad about it, though, knowing that all things have an end. So we went up the

Fraser River to the plant and delivered our fish. Our little fishing adventure was over. It was nice.

That voyage up around Vancouver Island to fish sardines was indeed our last trip. Byron's health deteriorated over the next three years and he died November 7, 2007. I have not fished since.

# ACKNOWLEDGEMENTS

**M**y fishing career spans the time from 1953 to 2004, with some interruptions, which is over fifty years for those who count. I fished on many boats with many skippers and I must acknowledge my debt to them. They are (with the vessels), in order of first to last: Arnie Wasden (*Jean W*), Walter Hunger (*Walter M*), Ronnie Myers (*Cedric A*), Vern Skogan (*Walter M, Northisle, W R Lord, Izumi II*), Boots Jolliffe (*Moresby III*), Freddy Jolliffe (*Barkley Sound, Vanisle*) and Byron Wright (*BC Maid, Prosperity*). Only the *Prosperity*, launched in 1990, is still fishing today.

None of my old skippers are currently fishing for a living and several are deceased, including my friend and partner, Byron Wright. So I am not apprehensive about revealing their knowledge and secrets, as their time and their fisheries (and mine) are now long past. In describing many of the various fisheries here I am sure they would have a different interpretation than mine. They looked at our sets from the behind the wheel, whereas I was mostly on the shore or in the skiff looking at the vessel and its net as we fished. As a beach man, I had plenty of time to reflect upon how the seine net was set at different times and in various locations on the coast and how and why it was done that way. Like a goalie in hockey I saw it all.

While I was mostly a beach man (sometimes cook and engineer and once all three), in later years I spent much time in the wheelhouse with my long-time friend and partner, Byron Wright, the captain of the *Prosperity*, and saw fishing operations from his perspective. Indeed we planned many seasons and sets together. So in a way I have seen the fisheries from both the beach and the wheelhouse. What I saw, remembered and recorded over the years is distilled here.

Fisheries historians are few and far between. One stands out: Alan Haig-Brown, who has chronicled the BC fisheries for many years. I have benefitted from his insights and his help in fishing matters for almost fifty years, since we were both at university so long ago.

I would be remiss in not thanking my family and my wife, Carol, who fished with me and who supported me in this endeavour and now gets to hear it all again. I had many good shipmates, but she is the best shipmate I ever had.

# INDEX

219